200 easy vegetarian
dishes

D0970843

hamlyn | all color cookbook

200 easy vegetarian dishes

Denise Smart

An Hachette UK Company
www.hachette.co.uk

First published in Great Britain in 2014 by Hamlyn
a division of Octopus Publishing Group Ltd
Endeavour House, 189 Shaftesbury Avenue
London WC2H 8JY
www.octopusbooksusa.com

Distributed in the US by Hachette Book Group USA
237 Park Avenue, New York NY 10017 USA

Distributed in Canada by Canadian Manda Group
165 Dufferin Street, Toronto, Ontario, Canada M6K 3H6

ISBN: 978-0-600-62825-5

Printed and bound in China

1 2 3 4 5 6 7 8 9 10

Standard level spoon and cup measurements
are used in all recipes.

Ovens should be preheated to the specified temperature—
if using a convection oven, follow the manufacturer's
instructions for adjusting the time and temperature.

Fresh herbs should be used unless otherwise stated.
Medium eggs should be used unless otherwise stated.
Freshly ground black pepper should be used unless
otherwise stated

The U.S. Food and Drug Administration advises that eggs
should not be consumed raw. This book contains some dishes
made with raw or lightly cooked eggs. It is prudent for
vulnerable people, such as pregnant and nursing mothers,
people with weakened immune systems, the elderly, babies,
and young children, to avoid uncooked or lightly cooked dishes
made with eggs. Once prepared, these dishes should be kept
refrigerated and used promptly.

This book includes dishes made with nuts and nut derivatives.
It is advisable for people with known allergic reactions to nuts
and nut derivatives or those who may be potentially vulnerable
to these allergies, such as pregnant and nursing mothers,
people with weakened immune systems, the elderly, babies,
and children, to avoid dishes made with these. It is prudent
to check the labels of all prepared ingredients for the possible
inclusion of nut derivatives.

contents

introduction

introduction

The North American Vegetarian Society says vegetarians are: "people who abstain from eating all animal flesh including meat, poultry, fish and other sea animals." Some vegetarians eat eggs (ovo-vegetarian) or dairy products (lacto-vegetarian) or both (ovo-lacto vegetarian). A vegan, or total vegetarian, does not include eggs or dairy in their diet. People may follow a vegetarian diet for various reasons, including religious, social, lifestyle, moral, environmental, and health.

Today, being a vegetarian, cooking for a vegetarian in your family, or choosing to have a couple of meat-free days a week can be easier, with supermarkets and health food stores offering a range of ingredients for making tasty and satisfying vegetarian dishes. Many people perceive vegetarian cooking as being time-consuming and featuring heavy stews of beans and lentils, nut loaves, and omelets. This book aims to dispel that myth. It provides 200 recipes to help you create simple, flavorful vegetarian feasts, with inspirational ideas for easy, nutritious dishes for breakfast and brunch, appetizers and snacks, main dishes, soups and stews, salads and sides, breads and baking, and desserts. So there's sure to be something here to please all tastes, vegetarian and nonvegetarian alike.

ingredients

For vegetarians, avoiding certain products can be difficult. For example, animal fat and ingredients, such as gelatin, may be used in manufactured foods. Rennet, which is extracted from the stomach lining of cows, is often used in cheese making. Also, some jars of Indian-style sauces may contain shrimp. In many cases, there are vegetarian alternatives to these ingredients, so it is advisable to take time to read the ingredients on the food labels.

The following is a brief guide to the ingredients commonly used in the recipes.

dried and canned beans and other legumes

Gone are the days when you have to soak dried beans and legumes overnight. Cans of beans can make a nutritious speedy meal, just drain, rinse under cold water, and drain again well before using. It is worth keeping a good supply of the following in your pantry.

Red kidney beans These red beans make a popular choice for soups, stews, casseroles, and hot spicy dishes, such as Quick Vegetable Mole on page 146.

Black beans This member of the kidney bean family can be used in stews, soups, and salads or as a substitute for red kidney beans.

Cannellini beans These small, creamy white members of the kidney bean family are ideal for salads, such as the Cannellini & Green Bean Salad on page 158.

Lima beans These large, flattish, creamy white beans have a mild flavor and floury texture, and they absorb a lot of flavor. They are great cooked in stews or soups—for a quick lunch, try the Lima Bean & Vegetable Soup on page 142.

Dried red split lentils These lentils need no soaking and quickly cook down to a puree. They are commonly used in Indian-style dishes, such as the Spinach & Tomato Dhal on page 152.

Green and brown lentils Brown lentils are the most commonly used; both types are mostly found dry, but they need cooking in water for only 20–25 minutes without presoaking.

Chickpeas These look like small hazelnuts and have a nutty flavor. Featuring in Middle Eastern, Mediterranean, and Indian cooking, they are added to curries and stews or used in salads or dips, such as hummus. Try roasting them with spices, such as in Moroccan Spiced Chickpeas on page 44.

Soybeans These can be bought shelled and frozen, requiring just a few minutes' cooking. Delicious in salads, soups, or noodle dishes.

grains and rice

Here are some grains worth keeping on hand in your pantry—use whole grains where possible.

Quinoa This is actually a seed from South America, which has become popular during the past few years. It is high in protein, quick to cook, and has a chewy, slightly nutty flavor. It is also available in red and black. Quinoa is perfect for soaking up sauces, or why not start the day with a bowl of the Quinoa Porridge with Raspberries on page 36.

Bulgur wheat This whole-wheat grain is steam-dried and cracked, needing only a brief soaking before serving. It's popular in Middle Eastern cooking, the best-known example being the salad dish tabbouleh.

Couscous Originating from North Africa, couscous is the staple ingredient in the North African diet. These tiny granules are made from steamed and dried semolina formed into tiny pellets. Couscous is a popular alternative to rice and pasta, and has a light, fluffy texture that is a little bland in flavor but which readily soaks up the flavors of other ingredients. Serve it with the Moroccan-inspired Chickpea & Eggplant Stew on page 150, or for a change, try giant or whole-wheat couscous.

Rice While many people in the West think of rice as a simple side dish, rice is exciting when cooked as a meal in its own right and easily absorbs other flavors. The different cultivation techniques, as well as crossbreeding of rice, have resulted in thousands of varieties, including sticky rices, wild rices, and fragrant rices. Keep a selection of brown, jasmine, long-grain, risotto and short-grain rice. Grown on hillsides, in soil, or in irrigated waters, either deep or shallow.

pasta and noodles

Pasta is made from durum flour and eggs, and is available fresh and dried and in many shapes, such as penne, farfalle, fusilli, tagliatelle, spaghetti, and linguine, to name just a few. Stuffed pasta, such as ravioli and tortellini, are sold chilled in supermarkets filled with delicious vegetarian fillings, such as spinach and ricotta or pumpkin and goat cheese. Pasta makes a great accompaniment or a main dish. Gnocchi is a small potato dumpling for tossing in sauce or butter.

Noodles can be made from rice, wheat, or buckwheat and are available fresh or dried. You can buy a huge selection of noodles in your supermarket or from Asian food stores. Varieties include soba, udon, somen, cellophane, ramen, vermicelli, or flat rice noodles. Use them in soups and stir-fries, or as an accompaniment to a main dish.

food to keep in the refrigerator

Stock up on the following ingredients regularly, and you will be ready to cook up a whole range of tempting vegetarian dishes.

tofu

Also called bean curd, tofu is made from soybeans. It's extremely versatile and can be used in stir-fries, casseroles, and soups. Although it's bland in taste, with the addition of flavorings and marinades it can be delicious. Try the Tandoori Tofu Bites on page 58.

cheese

Cheese is a good source of protein for vegetarians, but always check the label to make sure that it is suitable for vegetarians and doesn't contain animal rennet. Some hard cheeses are still made with animal rennet, although increasingly cheese is being made with "microbial enzymes," widely used in the industry because they are a consistent and inexpensive coagulant.

The term "microbial enzyme" means that it is a synthetically developed coagulant, while the term "vegetable rennet" indicates one derived from a vegetable source. Soft cheeses, such as cream cheese and cottage cheese, are manufactured without rennet. Some cottage cheeses, however, may contain gelatin, which is derived from animal sources.

The following cheeses are suitable for vegetarians; keep them in the refrigerator:

Goat cheese Made from goat milk, this cheese has a tangy flavor and can be either soft and creamy or it is bought hard, so is suitable for grating.

11

Feta This creamy, crumbly white Greek cheese is traditionally made from sheep milk or a mixture of sheep and goat milk, but is now sometimes made using cow milk. It has a salty flavor and is perfect in salads, with couscous or pasta.

Mozzarella An Italian fresh or unripened cheese traditionally made from water buffalo milk around the Naples area in Italy. A firm but creamy cheese, it tastes like fresh milk with a slightly sour edge. It melts well and has a unique stretchiness, making it the classic pizza-topping cheese. Used in Margherita Biscuit-Crust Pizza, page 186.

Cheddar Made from cow milk, a lot of cheddar is now produced using vegetarian rennet. Mature cheddar has great flavor.

Vegetarian Parmesan-style cheese This is a great vegetarian alternative to Parmesan cheese, for use in risottos or pasta dishes.

Taleggio From Northern Italy, this mild, whole cow milk cheese has a soft texture and a fruity, creamy character. It is used in Macaroni & Cheese with Spinach on page 98.

Ricotta This soft Italian curd cheese is made from whey, which is drained and then lightly "cooked." It is creamy with a slightly grainy texture and delicate flavor. Relatively low in fat, it is used in many Italian dishes.

other useful refrigerator ingredients
Eggs Keep a mixture of large and extra-large eggs. Always buy free-range.

Vegetables Keep a good selection of green leafy vegetables, bell peppers, onions, tomatoes, carrots, sweet potatoes, parsnips, squashes, potatoes, and mushrooms.

Store-bought puff pastry Fresh or frozen.

Fresh pasta, noodles, and gnocchi

Milk, yogurt, butter, and crème fraîche or cream. Make sure the yogurt does not contain gelatin.

flavorings & sauces

A simple way of adding exciting flavors to meals is using a selection of herbs and spices (fresh or dried), pastes, or sauces and condiments from a jar. Have the following to hand:

Harissa paste A fiery North African paste that is orangey red in color. A mixture of bell peppers, dried red chiles, garlic, caraway seeds, ground cumin, and coriander, tomato paste, salt, and olive oil. Used as a condiment or as an ingredient, it provides a real flavor boost.

Moroccan and Middle Eastern spice mixes Such as baharat, zahtar, and ras-el-hanout.

Curry sauces Such as tikka and korma. Be careful when choosing Thai-style sauces, because many of these may contain shrimp.

Dark and light soy sauce Great for adding saltiness to a dish instead of Thai fish sauce.

Chipotle paste A smoky chili paste used in Mexican dishes.

Nuts and seeds Pine nuts, cashew nuts, walnuts, and peanuts. Sunflower seeds, pumpkin seeds, and flaxseed.

Oils Sunflower, peanut, olive, and sesame oils.

Vegetable stock Use bouillon cubes or powder, or fresh vegetable stock or broth.

Spices A selection, including ground coriander, ground cumin, cumin seeds, paprika, smoked paprika, curry powder, chili powder, turmeric, mustard seeds.

Dried herbs Dried mixed herbs and oregano.

Fresh herbs Such as cilantro, basil, parsley, chives, thyme, rosemary, and tarragon. Grow in flowerpots on your windowsill or in your backyard.

Mustard Whole-grain, Dijon, and English.

Ketchup, wasabi paste, sweet chili sauce

Diced and plum tomatoes, coconut milk

Lemon grass, kaffir lime leaves, and curry leaves.

ensuring a balanced diet

A vegetarian diet can supply all the nutrients needed for health and vitality, and eating vegetarian can make it easier to achieve the desired daily consumption of fresh fruit and vegetables. Eat from the following groups:

protein

This can come from many sources, the main ones are as follows. Legumes (peas, beans, and lentils) are an excellent and inexpensive source of protein and also contain minerals such as iron, zinc, and calcium. Soybean products, which include tofu, as well as vegetarian protein products, which are available as meat-free ground beef, meatballs, and patties, and chicken cutlets and entrées. The third source is free-range eggs and dairy products, nuts and seeds. These contain zinc, calcium, and iron.

fruit and vegetables

Aim to eat at least five portions a day, where one portion weighs about 3 oz. Try to choose a wide variety of fruit and vegetables in different colors, which will provide a balanced mixture of nutrients.

carbohydrate-rich foods

Potatoes, pasta, rice, and beans provide sustained energy from carbohydrates, as well as the B vitamins and fiber. One-third of your food intake should be made up of carbohydrate, so try to eat one food from this group each meal.

dairy products or alternatives

These are needed for protein and calcium. At least three portions should be eaten each day, where one portion is a glass of milk, ⅔ cup of yogurt, or a 1 oz piece of cheese. Alternatives include rice milk, dried figs, nuts, green vegetables, and soybean products, such as tofu.

vitamins and minerals

Iron is vital for the maintenance of healthy red blood cells and to prevent anemia. Vegetarian sources include eggs, leafy green vegetables, whole-wheat bread, molasses, dried fruit (especially apricots), beans, fortified breakfast cereals, pumpkin seeds, sesame and sunflower seeds, and peanut butter. Iron from vegetable sources is not as easily absorbed as that from animal sources. If eaten with food rich in vitamin C, the body's absorption of iron can be enhanced. Drink fruit juice with breakfast cereal, or squeeze fresh lemon juice on green vegetables and salads.

kitchen equipment

So you have the ingredients on hand and it's time to cook. All you need are a few items of kitchen equipment.

tools for the job

Pans The most important tool is a large, heavy skillet or wok. Make sure the skillet has a flameproof handle so that it can go from the stove top to under the broiler.

You will also need a selection of good-quality saucepans with lids in different sizes, as well as at least two baking sheets. A ridged grill pan is a good idea, too.

Knives Make sure you have at least two good-quality knives, a small one for paring and slicing and a larger one for chopping. Also keep a few cutting boards.

Food processor Invest in a good-quality food processor and blending up pastes, pestos, and soups, and chopping fruits and nuts will suddenly seem as easy as pie.

Bowls You will need a selection of sizes.

Colander and strainer You will need a good-size colander and a fine-meshed strainer to make family meals.

Grater One that you can hold comfortably, has many slicing options, and, most importantly, is sharp, will feel like a help instead of a hindrance, and microplanes are fantastic for quickly removing the zest from citrus fruits.

Measuring tools A set of standard measuring spoons and cups, along with a liquid measuring cup, are essential for measuring ingredients.

Other basic tools These include stirring spoons, slotted spoons, a vegetable peeler, wire whisk, and tongs.

get cooking!

With a stocked pantry and refrigerator, the correct equipment, and 200 recipes to choose from, you are now ready to go.

breakfast
& brunch

honey-roasted granola

Serves **4**

Preparation time **10 minutes**, plus cooling

Cooking time **25–30 minutes**

⅓ cup **honey**

2 tablespoons **sunflower oil**

2¾ cups **rolled oats**

½ cup coarsely chopped **hazelnuts**

⅓ cup **blanched almonds**, coarsely chopped

⅓ cup **dried cranberries**

½ cup **dried blueberries**

Heat the honey and oil together gently in a small saucepan.

Mix the oats and nuts together thoroughly in a large bowl. Pour the warm honey mixture over the oat and nut mixture and stir well to combine.

Spread the mixture over a large nonstick baking sheet and bake in a preheated oven, at 300°F, for 20–25 minutes, stirring once, until golden.

Let the granola cool, then stir in the dried berries. Serve with skim milk or low-fat yogurt with live cultures and fresh fruit. Any remaining granola can be stored in an airtight container.

For oven-baked chocolate, almond & cherry granola, mix the honey and sunflower oil, warmed as above, with 2 tablespoons sifted unsweetened cocoa powder. Mix the rolled oats and ⅔ cup blanched almonds together in a large bowl. Pour the warm honey mixture over the oat and nut mixture and stir well to combine. Bake as above and let cool, then stir in ⅔ cup dried cherries. Serve with milk.

tomato, bell pepper & egg tortillas

Serves **4**
Preparation time **15 minutes**
Cooking time **25–30 minutes**

1 tablespoon **olive oil**
1 small **onion**, finely chopped
1 **garlic clove**, crushed
1 **mild green chile**, seeded
   and finely chopped
1 small **green bell pepper,**
   cored, seeded, and
   thinly sliced
1 small **red bell pepper,**
   cored, seeded, and thinly
   sliced
1 (14½ oz) can **diced**
   tomatoes
2 tablespoons **ketchup**
4 **eggs**
4 **corn tortillas**
smoked paprika, for
   sprinkling
salt and **black pepper**

Heat the oil in a large skillet with a lid, add the onion, garlic, chile, and bell peppers, and cook over medium heat, stirring frequently, for 10–15 minutes, until the bell peppers are soft. Stir in the tomatoes and ketchup and season with salt and black pepper. Bring to a boil, then simmer for 5 minutes, until thickened.

Make 4 shallow hollows in the tomato mixture with the back of a spoon and break an egg into each hollow. Cover the pan and cook over low heat for about 5 minutes, until just set.

Meanwhile, warm the tortillas according to the package directions. Place each tortilla on a warmed serving plate and carefully transfer the egg and tomato mixture onto each tortilla. Serve immediately, sprinkled with a little smoked paprika.

For breakfast mushroom quesadillas, heat 2 tablespoons olive oil in a large skillet, add 1 small chopped onion, 1 crushed garlic clove, and 1 finely chopped green chile, and cook gently for 2–3 minutes. Increase the heat, add 1 lb mixed mushrooms, trimmed and coarsely chopped, and cook for 4–5 minutes, until they start to release their juice. Stir in 1 teaspoon lime juice and 2 tablespoons chopped parsley and cook for another 5 minutes, until the mushrooms are tender. Meanwhile, heat a large, heavy skillet over medium heat, add 4 corn tortillas, and heat for 30 seconds on each side, until soft. Place a quarter of the mushroom mixture on one half of a tortilla, fold over, and press down. Turn over and cook until the tortilla is slightly crispy. Repeat with the remaining tortillas and mushroom mixture.

sunshine breakfast muffins

Makes **10**
Preparation time **10 minutes**
Cooking time **20–25 minutes**

2 cups **all-purpose flour**
1 tablespoon **baking powder**
1 cup **rolled oats**
1 cup chopped **dried apricots**
⅓ cup **dried cranberries**
2 tablespoons **mixed seeds**,
　such as sunflower, flaxseed,
　pumpkin, and hemp
¼ cup firmly packed **light
　brown sugar**
½ teaspoon **salt**
2 **eggs**, lightly beaten
¾ cup **milk**
⅓ cup **sunflower oil**
¼ cup **honey**

Line a 12-section muffin pan with 10 paper liners.

Sift together the flour and baking powder into a large bowl. Stir in the oats, dried fruits, seeds, sugar, and salt with a metal spoon.

Beat together the eggs, milk, oil, and honey in a small bowl. Pour the liquid ingredients over the dry ingredients and stir until only just combined; the batter should be lumpy and fairly runny.

Spoon the batter into the paper liners so that they are two-thirds full and bake on the top shelf of a preheated oven, at 375°F, for 20–25 minutes, until risen and golden.

Let cool in the pan for 5 minutes, then transfer to a wire rack to cool completely.

For banana breakfast muffins, follow the above recipe to make the muffin batter, using ¾ cup steel-cut oats in place of the oats and ⅓ cup golden raisins in place of the dried apricots and cranberries.

ricotta & blueberry pancakes

Serves **4**

Preparation time **10 minutes**

Cooking time **10–15 minutes**

1 cup **ricotta cheese**

½ cup **milk**

3 **extra-large eggs**, separated

¾ cup plus 1 tablespoon
   all-purpose flour

3 tablespoons **sugar**

1 teaspoon **baking powder**

finely grated zest of 1 **lemon**

1 cup **fresh blueberries**

unsalted butter, for frying

lemon juice or **maple syrup**,
   to serve

Beat the ricotta with the milk and egg yolks in a large bowl. Stir in the flour, sugar, baking powder, lemon zest, and blueberries until well combined.

Whisk the egg whites with a handheld electric mixer in a separate large, grease-free bowl until they form soft peaks, then gently fold into the ricotta mixture with a large metal spoon.

Heat a little butter in a heavy skillet over medium heat. Add about one-quarter of the batter to the pan to make 3–4 pancakes about 3 inches in diameter and cook for 1–2 minutes on each side, until golden and cooked through. Transfer the pancakes to a baking sheet and keep warm in a low oven while you repeat with the remaining batter, adding a little more butter to the pan as necessary.

Serve 3–4 pancakes per person, with lemon juice or maple syrup.

For pancakes with blueberry compote, put 1 ⅓ cups blueberries into a saucepan with 2 tablespoons sugar and 1 tablespoon lemon juice. Heat gently, stirring occasionally, until the blueberries start to burst and release their juice. Simmer for 2–3 minutes, until jammy. Meanwhile, prepare 8 pancakes from a store-bought pancake mixture, following the package directions. Serve hot with the warm compote.

goat cheese omelets

Serves **4**

Preparation time **10 minutes**

Cooking time **20 minutes**

¼ cup **olive oil**

3½ cups halved mixed **red
and yellow cherry tomatoes**

a little **basil**, chopped, plus a
few sprigs to garnish

12 **eggs**

2 tablespoons **whole-grain
mustard**

4 tablespoons **butter**

4 oz **soft goat cheese**, diced

salt and **black pepper**

watercress or **mâche**,
to garnish

Heat the oil in a skillet, add the tomatoes, and cook over medium heat for 2–3 minutes, until softened (you may have to do this in 2 batches). Add the basil and season to taste with salt and black pepper, then transfer to a bowl and keep warm.

Beat the eggs with the mustard in a large bowl and season with salt and black pepper.

Melt one-quarter of the butter in an omelet pan or small skillet over medium heat until it stops foaming, then swirl in one-quarter of the egg mixture. Fork over the omelet so that it cooks evenly. As soon as it is set on the bottom (but still a little runny in the middle), dot with one-quarter of the goat cheese and cook for another 30 seconds. Carefully slide the omelet onto a warmed plate, folding it in half as you do so. Keep warm.

Repeat with the remaining mixture to make another 3 omelets. Serve with the tomatoes, garnished with watercress and basil sprigs.

oven-baked sausage brunch

Serves **2**

Preparation time **10 minutes**

Cooking time **30 minutes**

1 tablespoon **sunflower oil**

4 **vegetarian sausages**

2 **russet potatoes**, scrubbed
   and cut into ½ inch cubes

4 mini **portobello
   mushrooms**, trimmed

2 **tomatoes**, halved

2 **extra-large eggs**

black pepper

Heat the oil in a nonstick ovenproof dish or roasting pan in a preheated oven, at 400°F, until hot.

Add the sausages and potatoes to the hot oil and turn to coat in the oil. Cook in the oven for 10 minutes.

Remove the dish from the oven, add the mushrooms and tomatoes, and turn with the sausages and potatoes to coat in the oil. Return to the oven and cook for another 10–12 minutes, until the potatoes are golden and the sausages are cooked through.

Make 2 separate spaces in the baked mixture and break an egg into each. Return to the oven and cook for another 3–4 minutes, until the eggs are softly set. Grind some black pepper over the top and serve immediately.

For sausage & tomato tortilla, cook 2 vegetarian sausages under a preheated medium broiler for about 10 minutes, turning occasionally, until cooked through. Let cool slightly, then slice thickly. Meanwhile, boil 8 oz thickly sliced new potatoes in a saucepan of boiling water for 6–8 minutes, until tender, then drain well. Heat 1 tablespoon sunflower oil in a small skillet with a flameproof handle, add the sausages and potatoes, and cook for 2–3 minutes. Stir in 4 halved cherry tomatoes. Beat 3 eggs together, season well with salt and black pepper, and pour the eggs over the sausage mixture. Cook over low heat for 8–10 minutes, until just set. Sprinkle with ¼ cup shredded cheddar cheese, place the pan under a preheated high broiler, and cook for 2–3 minutes, until the tortilla is golden brown on top and set. Serve cut into wedges.

mixed berry smoothie

Serves **2**
Preparation time **5 minutes**

1 small ripe **banana**,
  coarsely chopped
1½ cups **fresh mixed**
  berries, such as raspberries,
  blueberries, and strawberries
1 cup **low-fat** or **fat-free**
  vanilla yogurt with
  live cultures
about ⅔ cup **low-fat milk**

Put the banana into a blender with the berries, yogurt, and milk and blend until thick and smooth, adding a little more milk if you prefer a thinner consistency.

Divide the smoothie between 2 glasses and serve immediately.

For banana, oat & honey smoothie, put 1 coarsely chopped ripe banana into a blender with 1 tablespoon each honey and rolled oats. Add 1¼ cups low-fat milk and blend until smooth. Divide the smoothie between 2 glasses and serve.

potato cakes with mushrooms

Serves **2**

Preparation time **15 minutes**

Cooking time **12 minutes**

1 tablespoon **olive oil**

2 tablespoons **unsalted butter**

2 **shallots**, finely chopped

8 oz **mixed mushrooms**, such as cremini, portobello, and button, trimmed and sliced

2 **garlic cloves**, chopped

1 tablespoon freshly squeezed **lemon juice**

2 tablespoons chopped **flat leaf parsley**

2 **extra-large eggs**

4 **potato pancakes**, prepared from a mix according to package directions

salt and **black pepper**

1 tablespoon chopped **chives**, to garnish

Heat the oil with the butter in a skillet over high heat. Reduce the heat slightly, add the shallots and mushrooms, and sauté for 6 minutes, stirring occasionally, until the mushrooms are golden. Stir in the garlic and cook, stirring, for 1 minute.

Add the lemon juice to the mushroom mixture and season with salt and black pepper.

Remove the skillet from the heat and stir in the parsley. Keep warm while you poach the eggs.

Fill a separate skillet halfway with water and bring to a simmer. Break in the eggs and cook for 3 minutes.

Place 2 potato pancakes on each warmed serving plate and top with the mushroom mixture, then the eggs. Sprinkle with the chives and serve immediately.

For potato hash browns with baked eggs & tomatoes, put 8 frozen potato hash browns in a roasting pan with 12 cherry tomatoes and drizzle with 1 tablespoon olive oil. Cook in a preheated oven, at 400°F, for 10 minutes. Remove from the oven and turn the hash browns over. Return to the oven and cook for another 6 minutes, until golden. Break 2 eggs into the roasting pan and return to the oven for 2–3 minutes or until the eggs are just set. Put 4 hash browns on each warmed serving plate, divide the roasted tomatoes among the plates, and add a baked egg to each.

scrambled eggs with asparagus

Serves **2**
Preparation time **10 minutes**
Cooking time **5 minutes**

4 **extra-large eggs**
¼ cup **light cream**
6 **asparagus spears**, woody
   ends removed
1 tablespoon **butter**
2 oz **soft goat cheese**, diced
4 slices of **challah bread**,
   toasted or 4 **croissants**,
   halved and warmed
salt and **black pepper**

Beat the eggs and cream together in a bowl and season with salt and black pepper.

Steam the asparagus spears for 4–5 minutes until tender.

Meanwhile, melt the butter in a small saucepan, add the egg mixture, and cook over low heat, stirring with a wooden spoon, until softly set. Remove from the heat and stir in the goat cheese.

Serve the scrambled eggs on the toasted challah bread or croissants with the steamed asparagus.

For cheese & watercress scrambled eggs, follow the recipe above to prepare and cook the scrambled eggs, then stir in ½ cup shredded sharp cheddar cheese, omitting the goat cheese. Meanwhile, halve 2 English muffins, then toast and butter. Remove the scrambled eggs from the heat and stir in a large handful of chopped watercress or mâche. Divide the mixture between the muffins and serve immediately.

quinoa porridge with raspberries

Serves **2**
Preparation time **5 minutes**
Cooking time **25–30 minutes**

2½ cups **milk**
⅔ cup **quinoa**
2 tablespoons **sugar**
½ teaspoon **ground
  cinnamon**
1 cup **fresh raspberries**
2 tablespoons **mixed seeds**,
  such as sunflower, flaxseed,
  pumpkin, and hemp
2 tablespoons **honey**

Bring the milk to a boil in a small saucepan. Add the quinoa and return to a boil. Reduce the heat to low, cover, and simmer for about 15 minutes, until three-quarters of the milk has been absorbed.

Stir the sugar and cinnamon into the pan, replace the lid, and cook for 8–10 minutes or until almost all the milk has been absorbed and the quinoa is tender.

Spoon the porridge into 2 bowls, then top with the raspberries, sprinkle with the seeds, and drizzle with the honey. Serve immediately.

For quinoa & maple syrup pancakes, mix together 1¼ cups cooked quinoa, 1 lightly beaten, extra-large egg, 1 cup all-purpose flour, 2 teaspoons baking powder, ½ teaspoon each of ground cinnamon and salt, 1 cup milk, and 2 tablespoons maple syrup in a large bowl until well combined. Melt a little butter in a skillet, add separate heaping tablespoonfuls of the batter, and cook for 2–3 minutes on each side, until golden brown. Serve with maple syrup and fresh berries.

banana & buttermilk pancakes

Serves **4**
Preparation time **10 minutes**
Cooking time **20 minutes**

1 cup **all-purpose flour**
pinch of **salt**
1 teaspoon **baking powder**
1 cup **buttermilk**
1 **egg**
2 small **bananas**, thinly sliced
1 tablespoon **vegetable oil**

To serve
1 **banana**, sliced
¼ cup chopped **pecans**
2 tablespoons **maple syrup**

Sift together the flour, salt, and baking powder into a large bowl, then make a well in the center.

Beat the buttermilk and egg together in a small bowl, add to the well, and gradually beat in the flour mixture from around the sides to make a smooth batter. Stir in the sliced bananas.

Heat a large, nonstick skillet over medium heat. Dip a scrunched-up piece of paper towel into the oil and use to wipe over the skillet. Drop 3 large tablespoonfuls of the batter into the pan to make 3 pancakes, spreading the batter out slightly with the spoon. Cook for 2–3 minutes, until bubbles start to appear on the surface and the underside is golden brown, then flip over and cook for another 2 minutes. Transfer the pancakes to a baking sheet and keep warm in a low oven while you repeat with the remaining oil and batter.

Serve 3 pancakes per person, topped with the extra sliced banana, sprinkled with the chopped nuts, and drizzled with the maple syrup.

For peanut butter & banana breakfast shakes, coarsely chop 4 ripe bananas and put into a blender with 3 cups cold milk and ¼ cup chunky peanut butter. Blend until smooth, then divide among 4 glasses and serve immediately.

fruit & nut bars

Makes **8**
Preparation time **10 minutes**
Cooking time **15 minutes**

1 stick **butter**
¼ cup **maple syrup**
2 tablespoons packed
  light brown sugar
1 cup **steel-cut oats**
1 cup **rolled oats**
½ cup chopped **mixed nuts**
1 cup chopped **mixed
  dried pitted fruit**, such
  as figs, dates, apricots,
  and cranberries
2 tablespoons **sunflower
  seeds**

Grease an 8 inch square nonstick baking pan lightly and line the bottom with nonstick parchment paper.

Melt the butter, syrup, and sugar together in a saucepan. Stir in all the remaining ingredients except the sunflower seeds, then press the mixture into the prepared pan.

Sprinkle with the sunflower seeds, then bake in a preheated oven, at 400°F, for 15 minutes or until golden. Cut into 8 bars and let cool.

For speedy oat bars, grease an 8 inch square nonstick baking pan lightly and line the bottom with nonstick parchment paper. Melt 1½ sticks unsalted butter with ¾ cup firmly packed dark brown sugar in a saucepan. Remove from the heat and stir through 1½ cups steel-cut oats. Press the mixture into the prepared pan and bake in a preheated oven, at 350°F, for 15 minutes. Cut into 12 bars and let cool.

appetizers & snacks

moroccan spiced chickpeas

Serves **4**
Preparation time **5 minutes**
Cooking time **35–40 minutes**

2 (15 oz) cans **chickpeas**,
   drained and rinsed
1 tablespoon **olive oil**
1 tablespoon **rose**
   harissa paste
1 tablespoon **Moroccan** or
   Middle Eastern spice mix,
   such as baharat
½ teaspoon **salt**

Dry the chickpeas on paper towels to remove any
excess water.

Mix all the remaining ingredients together in a large
bowl. Add the chickpeas and toss in the spice mix
to coat.

Spread the chickpeas out in a single layer on a rimmed
baking sheet and roast in a preheated oven, at 400°F,
for 35–40 minutes, until a deep golden color. Let cool
before serving.

For Indian spiced roasted mixed nuts, put
1 tablespoon sunflower oil in a small bowl and stir in
1 tablespoon medium curry powder and 1 teaspoon
cumin seeds. Add 2 cups mixed raw unsalted nuts,
such as cashew nuts, macadamia nuts, and almonds,
and turn to coat in the spice mix. Spread out in a
single layer on a nonstick baking sheet and roast
in a preheated oven, at 350°F, for 10 minutes, shaking
once, until lightly golden. Remove from the oven,
sprinkle with 1 teaspoon sea salt, and let cool.
Serve in bowls as a snack.

zucchini & mint fritters

Serves **4**

Preparation time **10 minutes**

Cooking time **18 minutes**

3 **zucchini**, coarsely grated

4 **scallions**, chopped

¼ cup chopped **mint**

1 cup **all-purpose flour**

1 teaspoon **baking powder**

2 **eggs**, lightly beaten

½ cup **ricotta cheese**

olive oil, for frying

salt and **black pepper**

lemon-flavored mayonnaise,
  to serve

Mix together the zucchini, scallions, mint, flour, and baking powder in a large bowl, then stir in the eggs. Mix well, season with salt and black pepper, then gently fold in the ricotta.

Heat a little oil in a large skillet. Add 4 separate heaping tablespoonfuls of the batter, flatten slightly, and cook for about 3 minutes on each side, until golden. Transfer the fritters to a baking sheet and keep warm in a low oven while you repeat with the remaining batter, adding a little more oil to the pan as necessary.

Serve the fritters immediately with a spoonful of lemon-flavored mayonnaise.

For feta & zucchini fritters, follow the recipe above to make the fritters, using 1 cup crumbled feta cheese in place of the ricotta. Cook as above and serve with store-bought tomato salsa instead of the mayonnaise.

vegetable spring rolls

Makes **12**
Preparation time **25 minutes**
Cooking time **12–15 minutes**

6 sheets of **phyllo pastry**,
   defrosted if frozen
2 tablespoons **butter**, melted
sweet chili dipping sauce,
   to serve

Filling

1 cup **bean sprouts**
1 cup shredded **cabbage**
1 **carrot**, cut into thin strips
½ **red bell pepper**, cored,
   seeded, and thinly sliced
6 **scallions**, thinly sliced
1 **garlic clove**, crushed
1 inch piece of **fresh ginger
   root**, peeled and grated
1 tablespoon **dark soy sauce**

Mix all the filling ingredients together in a large bowl.

Lay the sheets of phyllo pastry on top of one another in a pile on a cutting board and cut in half.

Brush the edges of 1 piece of phyllo with a little of the melted butter. Place some of the filling on the bottom edge. Fold in the ends and roll up. Repeat with the remaining phyllo and filling.

Place the rolls on a baking sheet and brush with melted butter. Bake in a preheated oven, at 375°F, for 12–15 minutes, until golden. Serve hot with sweet chili dipping sauce.

For spinach & ricotta phyllo tarts, brush 4 sections of a muffin pan with olive oil. Take sixteen 5 inch squares of phyllo pastry and brush 1 square with olive oil, then place another at an angle on top to produce a star shape and brush with a little more oil. Repeat with another 2 squares. Use the layered phyllo to line an oiled muffin section. Repeat with the remaining phyllo squares. Put ½ cup ricotta cheese into a small bowl and stir in ¼ cup shredded cheddar cheese, 1 lightly beaten egg, and a pinch of grated nutmeg, then season well with salt and black pepper. Stir in 2 cups chopped baby spinach leaves. Fill the tart shells with the ricotta mixture and bake in a preheated oven, at 350°F, for 25 minutes, until golden.

cajun popcorn

Serves **6**
Preparation time **5 minutes**
Cooking time about **5 minutes**

2 tablespoons **corn oil**
½ cup **popping corn**
1 stick **salted butter**
2 tablespoons **Cajun spice mix**

Heat the oil in a saucepan until almost smoking and add the corn so that it forms a layer 1–2 grains deep. Cover and shake the pan so that the corn becomes coated in the oil. Reduce the heat to medium and let cook for about 2 minutes while the corn is popping.

Shake the pan carefully once the popping subsides, then let cook for another few seconds. Once the popping quietens down again, turn off the heat so that the popcorn doesn't burn.

Meanwhile, place the butter and spice mix in a small saucepan and heat over low heat, stirring frequently, until melted.

Transfer the popcorn to a large bowl, drizzle with the spiced butter, and stir until all the popcorn is coated in the butter. Serve immediately.

For toffee popcorn, cook the popcorn as above. Meanwhile, put 4 tablespoons of butter and ¼ cup firmly packed light brown sugar with 3 tablespoons light corn syrup in a saucepan. Stir together over medium heat until the butter has melted and the sugar has dissolved. Place the popcorn in a large bowl, drizzle with the toffee sauce, and stir until all the popcorn is coated in the sauce. Stop stirring when the sauce has cooled and is beginning to set. Let stand until cool enough to eat.

roasted red pepper & walnut dip

Serves **4–6**

Preparation time **10 minutes**, plus cooling

Cooking time **10 minutes**

4 large **red bell peppers**

¾ cup **walnut pieces**

juice of **1 lemon**

1 tablespoon **pomegranate molasses**

½ teaspoon **chili paste**

1 tablespoon **olive oil**

salt and **black pepper**

To serve

pomegranate seeds

mint leaves

flatbreads (optional)

Cut each bell pepper into quarters and remove and discard the core and seeds. Place skin side up under a preheated high broiler and cook until the skin is blackened. Transfer to a food bag and let stand until cool enough to handle.

Remove and discard the blackened skins from the bell peppers and place the flesh on paper towels to remove the excess moisture.

Put the walnuts into a food processor and process until finely ground. Add all the remaining ingredients, then process until smooth.

Scrape the mixture into a bowl and season to taste with salt and black pepper.

Serve garnished with pomegranate seeds and mint leaves, with warmed flatbreads, if desired.

For grilled haloumi, pomegranate & arugula salad, mix together 1 cup pomegranate seeds, 1 seeded and finely chopped small red chile, ½ small red onion, finely chopped, 2 teaspoons pomegranate molasses or balsamic vinegar, the finely grated zest and juice of 1 lime, and ¼ cup chopped fresh cilantro. Divide 4 cups arugula leaves among 4 bowls and add ¾ cup chopped roasted red peppers, either home prepared or from a jar. Heat a ridged grill pan or large skillet over medium-high heat. When hot, add 1 lb sliced haloumi cheese or Muenster cheese and cook, in batches, for about 1 minute on each side. Arrange the cheese over the arugula, then drizzle with the pomegranate seed mixture. Serve immediately.

japanese-style guacamole

Serves **4**

Preparation time **15 minutes**

2 ripe **avocados**

juice of 2 small **limes**

1–2 teaspoons **wasabi paste**,
to taste

4 **scallions**, finely chopped

1 tablespoon **sesame seeds**,
toasted, plus extra
for sprinking

1 teaspoon **mirin (Japanese
rice wine)**

1 teaspoon finely chopped
pickled ginger

sesame seeds, for sprinkling

prawn or **rice crackers**,
to serve

Cut the avocados in half and remove and discard the pits. Peel off the skin and coarsely chop the flesh. Put into a bowl and coarsely mash with a fork.

Stir in the lime juice, wasabi, scallions, sesame seeds, and mirin.

Transfer to a serving bowl and sprinkle with the pickled ginger and extra sesame seeds. Serve immediately, with rice crackers for dipping.

For avocado & rice salad with wasabi dressing,
put 1 ⅓ cups cooled, freshly cooked long-grain rice in a bowl and stir in 1 pitted, peeled, and chopped avocado, ½ cup thinly sliced radishes, ⅔ cup cooked edamame, and ½ cucumber, halved lengthwise, seeded and thinly sliced. Whisk together 1 tablespoon each of mirin (Japanese rice wine) and toasted sesame oil, 2 teaspoons lime juice, and 1 teaspoon wasabi paste, season to taste with salt and black pepper, and then pour the dressing over the salad. Toss gently and serve immediately.

grilled greek-style sandwiches

Serves **2**
Preparation time **15 minutes**
Cooking time **4–6 minutes**

¼ small **red onion**,
   thinly sliced
8 **cherry tomatoes**, quartered
4 **pitted ripe black olives**,
   chopped
2 inch piece of **cucumber**,
   seeded and cut into
   small pieces
1 teaspoon **dried oregano**
⅓ cup crumbled **feta cheese**
1 teaspoon **lemon juice**
2 **seeded pita breads**
¼ cup shredded **cheddar
   cheese**
olive oil, for brushing
black pepper

Mix together the onion, tomatoes, olives, cucumber, oregano, and feta in a small bowl. Add the lemon juice, season to taste with black pepper, and gently mix.

Split each pita bread in half horizontally. Divide the feta mixture between the bottom halves of the pita breads, then add the cheddar. Cover with the top halves of the pita breads.

Brush a ridged grill pan with oil and heat over medium heat. When hot, add the sandwiches, press down gently with a spatula, and cook for 2–3 minutes on each side until golden and the cheese has melted. Serve immediately.

For Greek salad with toasted pita croutons, cut 4 ripe tomatoes into wedges and put into a bowl with ½ cucumber, seeded and chopped, ¼ red onion, thinly sliced, 8 Greek kalamata olives, and ⅔ cup crumbled feta cheese. Whisk together 2 tablespoons extra virgin olive oil, 1 tablespoon lemon juice, and 1 teaspoon dried oregano in a small bowl and season to taste with black pepper. Pour the dressing over the salad and toss gently. Lightly toast 2 whole-wheat pita breads, then cut into croutons. Divide the salad between 2 plates and sprinkle with the croutons.

tandoori tofu bites

Serves **4**
Preparation time **15 minutes**,
   plus standing and marinating
Cooking time **20–25 minutes**

13 oz **firm tofu**, drained
lemon wedges and **parsley**,
   to serve

Marinade
½ cup **plain Greek yogurt**
1 teaspoon peeled and grated
   fresh ginger root
1 **garlic clove**, crushed
1 tablespoon **tandoori masala**
1 teaspoon **garam masala**
1 teaspoon **ground coriander**
½ teaspoon **salt**
¼ teaspoon **ground turmeric**
2 tablespoons **lemon juice**

Place the tofu between 2 pieces of paper towels and set a cutting board or other weight on top. Let stand for at least 10 minutes to remove the excess water.

Remove the weight and paper towels, then cut the tofu into cubes.

Mix all the marinade ingredients together in a large nonmetallic bowl and stir in the tofu. Cover and let marinate for 1 hour.

Place the tofu pieces on a lightly oiled nonstick baking sheet and cook in a preheated oven, at 400°F, for 20–25 minutes, turning halfway through the cooking time.

Serve the tofu cubes with cocktail sticks for skewering, lemon wedges for squeezing over them, and parsley for a garnish.

For baked teriyaki tofu bites, follow the recipe above to remove the excess water from the tofu, then cut into cubes. For the marinade, mix together 2 tablespoons each of dark soy sauce and rice wine or dry sherry, 2 teaspoons peeled and chopped fresh ginger root, 1 teaspoon chopped garlic, and 1 tablespoon each of light brown sugar and sesame seeds in a large nonmetallic bowl. Stir in the tofu, cover, and let marinate for 30 minutes. Cook the tofu as above, then serve on toothpicks, garnished with shredded scallions.

smoky spanish tortilla

Serves **6–8**

Preparation time **10 minutes**

Cooking time **30–35 minutes**

2 tablespoons **olive oil**

1 large **onion**, thinly sliced

1 teaspoon **smoked paprika**,
    plus extra for sprinkling

4 **Yukon gold** or **white round
    potatoes**, scrubbed and
    thickly sliced

6 **eggs**

salt and **black pepper**

Heat 1 tablespoon of the oil in an 8 inch nonstick skillet with a flameproof handle and a lid, add the onion and smoked paprika, and cook gently for 4–5 minutes, until the onion has softened.

Add the potatoes and stir to coat in the onion and paprika mixture. Cover and cook for 15 minutes, turning once and shaking the pan from time to time, until tender.

Beat the eggs together in a large bowl and season with salt and black pepper. Add the potato and onion mixture and mix thoroughly.

Heat the remaining oil in the skillet, add the egg and potato mixture, and cook over low heat for 8–10 minutes, without stirring, until set.

Place the pan under a preheated high broiler and cook for 2–3 minutes, until the top of the tortilla is golden brown. Transfer to a board, sprinkle with a little extra smoked paprika, and serve cut into wedges.

For saffron potato tortilla, put 1 teaspoon saffron threads into a small heatproof bowl, then cover with 1 tablespoon boiling water and let steep while you cook the onion as above, omitting the paprika, and then adding the potatoes. Beat the eggs with the saffron and its steeping liquid, then continue as above.

fava bean hummus

Serves **4**
Preparation time **20 minutes**
Cooking time **4 minutes**

2⅔ cups **shelled fresh** or
 frozen fava beans
1 **garlic clove**, crushed
grated zest and juice of
 1 lemon
3 tablespoons **extra virgin
 olive oil**
4 oz **goat cheese**
8 slices of **ciabatta**, toasted
salt and **black pepper**
watercress leaves or **mâche**,
 to garnish

Cook the fava beans in a saucepan of boiling water for 4 minutes, until tender. Drain the beans, then refresh under cold running water and drain again. Slip the beans out of their gray skins, discarding the skins.

Put the beans into a food processor with the garlic and pulse until coarsely chopped. Add the lemon zest and juice and then, with the motor running, trickle in the oil through the feed tube. Process until smooth and season to taste with salt and black pepper.

Spread a little goat cheese on each slice of toasted ciabatta, top with the hummus, and serve garnished with watercress leaves or mâche.

For fava bean, mint & mozzarella salad, cook 1⅓ cups fava beans in boiling water and then refresh under cold running water and remove the skins as above. Put the beans into a large bowl and stir in the grated zest and juice of 1 lemon and 2 tablespoons each of chopped mint and olive oil. Cut 2 buffalo mozzarella balls in half and place each half in the center of a serving plate. Spoon the fava bean mixture over the top and serve immediately with plenty of freshly ground black pepper and a few mint leaves.

pea & mint falafels with mint dip

Serves **4**

Preparation time **20 minutes**,
  plus chilling

Cooking time **5–7 minutes**

1 cup **frozen peas**

1 (15 oz) can **chickpeas**,
  drained and rinsed, then
  drained again well

½ cup **fresh white bread
  crumbs**

1 **garlic clove**, crushed

1 **red** or **green chile**, seeded
  and finely chopped

1 tablespoon **ground cumin**

1 teaspoon **ground coriander**

¼ cup chopped **mint**

1 teaspoon **baking powder**

1 **egg**, lightly beaten

2 tablespoons **sunflower oil**

salt and **black pepper**

whole-wheat pita breads,
  to serve

Mint dip

½ cup **low-fat plain yogurt**

2 tablespoons chopped **mint**

¼ **cucumber**, finely chopped

Cook the peas in a saucepan of boiling water for 1 minute. Drain the peas, then refresh under cold running water and drain again thoroughly.

Put the peas into a food processor with the chickpeas, bread crumbs, garlic, chile, spices, mint, and salt and black pepper, then pulse until coarsely chopped. Add the baking powder and egg and pulse until well combined.

Divide and shape the chickpea mixture into golf ball-size balls, then flatten slightly. Cover and chill in the refrigerator for 30 minutes.

Heat the oil in a large skillet, add the falafels, and cook over medium heat for 2–3 minutes on each side until golden. Remove from the pan and drain on paper towels.

Meanwhile, mix together all the ingredients for the dip in a small bowl and season to taste with salt and black pepper.

Serve the falafels with the mint dip, along with warmed whole-wheat pita bread.

For chickpea falafels, put two (15 oz) cans chickpeas, drained and rinsed, then drained again well, into a food processor with all the other ingredients for the falafels above, omitting the peas and using 2 tablespoons each of chopped flat leaf parsley and chopped fresh cilantro in place of the mint. Continue as above.

refried bean quesadillas

Serves **2**

Preparation time **5 minutes**

Cooking time **4–6 minutes**

1 cup canned **refried beans**

2 **scallions**, chopped

⅓ cup drained canned **corn kernels**

1 tablespoon chopped **fresh cilantro**

2 **soft corn tortillas**

3 tablespoons **prepared fresh tomato salsa**, plus extra to serve

½ cup shredded **cheddar** or **Monterey Jack cheese**

olive oil, for brushing

Mix together the refried beans, scallions, corn kernels, and cilantro in a bowl.

Spread 1 tortilla with the bean mixture, top with the salsa, and sprinkle the cheese over the top. Cover with the remaining tortilla.

Brush a large skillet or ridged grill pan with oil and heat over medium heat. When hot, add the quesadilla and cook over medium heat for 2–3 minutes, pressing down with a spatula, until the cheese starts to melt.

Place a large plate over the pan and invert the quesadilla onto the plate. Return to the pan and cook on the other side for 2–3 minutes.

Remove from the pan and cut into wedges. Serve with tomato salsa.

For refried bean & cheese burritos, put 2 large soft corn tortillas into a single layer in an ovenproof dish. Mix together 1 (16 oz) can refried beans, 2 chopped scallions, ⅔ cup drained canned corn kernels, 1 cup shredded cheddar or Monterey Jack cheese, 2 tablespoons chopped fresh cilantro, and ⅓ cup prepared fresh tomato salsa in a large bowl. Divide the mixture between the tortillas, placing it down the center, and spoon another ¾ cup fresh tomato salsa and ½ cup shredded cheddar or Monterey Jack cheese over the top. Bake in a preheated oven, at 400°F, for about 15 minutes, until piping hot and the cheese is melted and bubbling.

encrusted boiled eggs

Makes **4**
Preparation time **25 minutes**,
    plus cooling
Cooking time **10 minutes**

6 **eggs**
1 tablespoon **sunflower oil**,
    plus 4 cups for deep-frying
1 small **onion**, finely chopped
1 **carrot**, shredded
1 (15 oz) can **red kidney
    beans**, drained and rinsed,
    then drained again well
1 (15 oz) can **chickpeas**,
    drained and rinsed, then
    drained again well
finely grated zest and juice of
    ½ **lemon**
1 tablespoon **garam masala**
1 tablespoon chopped **flat
    leaf parsley**
⅓ cup **all-purpose flour**
2 cups **fresh white bread
    crumbs**
salt and **black pepper**
salad greens, to serve

Cook 4 of the eggs in a saucepan of boiling water for
6 minutes. Drain, then cool under cold running water
and drain again. Let cool completely and shell.

Meanwhile, heat the 1 tablespoon oil in a skillet, add
the onion and carrot, and cook over medium heat for
3–4 minutes, until softened. Transfer to a large bowl.

Put the kidney beans, chickpeas, lemon zest and juice,
and garam masala into a food processor and process
until smooth. Add to the onion and carrot with the
parsley and mix together. Season to taste with salt
and black pepper.

Beat the remaining eggs together lightly in a small
bowl. Tip the flour and bread crumbs into 2 separate
bowls. Mold one-quarter of the chickpea mixture around
each egg. Coat in the flour, then the beaten egg, and
finally the bread crumbs.

Heat the oil for deep-frying in a deep fryer or deep
saucepan to 350–375°F, or until a cube of bread browns
in 60 seconds. Deep-fry the eggs for 2–3 minutes, until
golden. Remove with a slotted spoon and drain on paper
towels. Serve warm or cold with mixed salad greens.

For chili tomato jam, to serve as an accompaniment,
put 4 halved tomatoes, a 1 inch piece of fresh ginger
root, peeled and chopped, 2 crushed garlic cloves, and
2 seeded and chopped red chiles in a food processor
and process until smooth. Transfer to a saucepan and
add 1¼ cups firmly packed light brown sugar and
3 tablespoons red wine vinegar. Bring to a boil and
simmer, stirring occasionally, for 30–35 minutes, until
thickened. Let cool.

hot haloumi with fattoush salad

Serves **2**
Preparation time **10 minutes**
Cooking time **2–4 minutes**

2 teaspoons **olive oil**
8 oz **haloumi cheese**
  or **Muenster cheese**,
  thickly sliced

Fattoush salad
1 small **red bell pepper**,
  cored, seeded, and
  finely sliced
1 small **yellow bell pepper**,
  cored, seeded, and
  finely sliced
¾ cup chopped **cucumber**
1⅓ cups finely chopped
  scallions
2 tablespoons chopped **flat
  leaf parsley**
2 tablespoons chopped **mint**
2 tablespoons chopped **fresh
  cilantro**

Dressing
1 teaspoon **crushed garlic**
2 tablespoons **olive oil** or
  flaxseed oil
¼ cup **lemon juice**
salt and **black pepper**

Heat the oil in a nonstick skillet, add the cheese, and cook over medium–high heat for 1–2 minutes on each side, until golden brown. Remove from the pan and keep warm.

Put the bell peppers, cucumber, scallions, and herbs into a bowl and stir to combine.

Make the dressing. Mix the garlic with the oil and lemon juice and season to taste with salt and black pepper.

Pour the dressing over the salad and toss lightly to mix. Serve with the warm cheese.

main dishes

lentil & parsnip casserole

Serve **6**

Preparation time **20 minutes**

Cooking time **45 minutes**

1 tablespoon **sunflower oil**

1 large **onion**, chopped

2 **celery sticks**, finely sliced

4 **carrots**, chopped

8 oz **cremini mushrooms**, trimmed and chopped

2 (15 oz) cans **green lentils in water**, drained, or 2 cups **dried green lentils**, cooked

1 (14½ oz) can **diced tomatoes**

1 tablespoon **tomato paste**

1¼ cups **vegetable stock**

2 teaspoons **dried mixed herbs**

4 **parsnips**, peeled and chopped

4 **Yukon gold** or **russet potatoes**, peeled and chopped

2 tablespoons **milk**

2 tablespoons **butter**

½ cup shredded **sharp cheddar cheese**

salt and **black pepper**

Heat the oil in a large saucepan, add the onion, celery, and carrots, and cook for 3–4 minutes, until softened. Increase the heat, stir in the mushrooms, and cook for another 3 minutes, stirring occasionally.

Add the lentils, tomatoes, tomato paste, and stock. Bring to a boil, then simmer, uncovered, for 15 minutes. Season to taste with salt and black pepper. Transfer to a 2 quart ovenproof dish.

Meanwhile, cook the parsnips and potatoes in a large saucepan of lightly salted boiling water for 20 minutes or until tender.

Drain the root vegetables and return to the pan. Mash with the milk and butter, and season to taste with salt and black pepper.

Spoon the mashed poatoes and parsnips over the lentil mixture and sprinkle with the cheese. Bake in a preheated oven, at 375°F, for 20 minutes, until golden and bubbling.

For lentil casserole with mashed sweet potatoes & goat cheese, prepare the lentil filling as above. Cook 6 sweet potatoes, peeled and chopped, in a large saucepan of boiling water for about 15 minutes or until tender. Drain, return to the pan, and mash with the milk and butter as above. Stir in ½ cup shredded hard goat cheese. Pile on top of the lentil mixture and bake as above.

beet & squash spaghetti

Serves **4**
Preparation time **10 minutes**
Cooking time **10 minutes**

12 oz **dried spaghetti**
  or **fusilli**
1½ cups **fine green beans**
½ **butternut squash**,
  peeled, seeded, and cut
  into ½ inch dice
¼ cup **olive oil**
6 **raw beets**, peeled and cut
  into ½ inch dice
½ cup **walnuts**, crushed
5 oz **goat cheese**, diced
2 tablespoons **lemon juice**
salt
vegetarian Parmesan-style
  cheese, to serve (optional)

Cook the pasta in a large saucepan of lightly salted boiling water according to the package directions, until al dente. Add the beans and squash for the final 2 minutes of cooking time.

Meanwhile, heat the oil in a large skillet, add the beets, and cook, stirring occasionally, for 10 minutes, until cooked but still firm.

Drain the pasta and vegetables, add to the skillet, and toss with the cooked beet, walnuts, and goat cheese.

Sprinkle the lemon juice over the pasta and serve immediately with a bowl of grated vegetarian Parmesan-style cheese, if desired.

For baby carrot & squash spaghetti, toss the butternut squash and 4 peeled garlic cloves in ¼ cup olive oil in a roasting pan and roast in a preheated oven, at 475°F, for about 40 minutes, until softened. Meanwhile, cook the pasta as above. At the same time, cook 1 lb baby carrots in a separate saucepan of boiling water for about 5 minutes, until tender. Drain the pasta and carrots and return to the pasta pan. Add the roasted squash and garlic with 1 cup diced havarti or dolcelatte cheese instead of the goat cheese and toss well. Sprinkle with the lemon juice and serve hot.

red onion & goat cheese tart

Serves **4**
Preparation time **15 minutes**,
  plus cooling
Cooking time **40 minutes**

2 tablespoons **unsalted
  butter**
4 large **red onions**,
  thinly sliced
1 teaspoon packed **light
  brown sugar**
2 tablespoons chopped
  thyme, plus a few extra
  leaves to garnish
2 teaspoons **balsamic vinegar**
1 sheet of **store-bought puff
  pastry**, defrosted if frozen
2 (4 oz) **goat cheese logs**,
  each sliced into 4

Melt the butter in a large skillet, add the onions, sugar, and chopped thyme, and cook gently for 20 minutes, stirring occasionally, until the onions start to caramelize. Stir in the vinegar and cook for 1 minute. Let the mixture cool slightly.

Unroll the pastry sheet and place on a nonstick baking sheet. Using a sharp knife, score a line along each side of the sheet, 1 inch from the edge, being careful not to cut all the way through the pastry.

Spoon the caramelized onions over the pastry, within the scored border, then top with the goat cheese slices.

Bake in a preheated oven, at 400°F, for 20 minutes, until the pastry is risen and golden. Serve garnished with a few thyme leaves.

For ricotta & cherry tomato tart, prepare the puff pastry as above. Beat together 1 cup ricotta cheese, ¼ cup grated cheddar cheese, 2 extra-large eggs, and 2 tablespoons shredded basil in a bowl until well combined. Season with a little salt and black pepper. Spoon the mixture over the pastry, within the scored border, then top with 16 halved cherry tomatoes. Bake as above.

feta, herb & arugula frittata

Serves **2**
Preparation time **5 minutes**
Cooking time **8–10 minutes**

4 **eggs**, beaten
2 tablespoons **chopped fresh herbs**, such as chives, chervil, and parsley
1 tablespoon **heavy cream**
1 tablespoon **olive oil**
1 small **red onion**, finely sliced
½ **red bell pepper**, cored, seeded, and finely sliced
⅔ cup crumbled **feta cheese**
large handful of **arugula leaves**
salt and **black pepper**

Beat together the eggs, herbs, and cream in a bowl, and season with salt and black pepper.

Heat the oil in a nonstick skillet with a flameproof handle, add the onion and red pepper, and cook over medium heat for 3–4 minutes, until just softened.

Pour in the egg mixture and cook for about 3 minutes, until almost set, then sprinkle with the feta.

Place the pan under a preheated high broiler and cook for 2–3 minutes, until the top of the tortilla is golden brown. Top with the arugula and serve.

For potato & goat cheese frittata, beat together the eggs, herbs, and cream, then season as above. Add 5 oz new potatoes, cooked and sliced, to the egg mixture and cook as above. Arrange 4 slices of firm goat cheese over the frittata and finish cooking under a preheated high broiler. Serve with a large handful of arugula leaves.

pasta with fennel & arugula

Serves **2**
Preparation time **10 minutes**
Cooking time **15 minutes**

1 tablespoon **olive oil**
1 **fennel bulb**, trimmed and
 thinly sliced
1 **garlic clove**, chopped
½ cup **dry white wine**
¼ cup **crème fraîche** or
 heavy cream
grated zest and juice of
 1 small **lemon**
2 cups **arugula leaves**
8 oz **fresh tagliatelle** or
 pappardelle
salt and **black pepper**
grated **vegetarian Parmesan-
 style cheese**, to serve

Heat the oil in a skillet, add the fennel and garlic, and cook gently for about 10 minutes, until the fennel is soft and golden.

Add the wine to the pan and cook until reduced by half. Stir in the crème fraîche or cream, lemon zest and juice, and arugula and cook, stirring, until the arugula has wilted. Season to taste with salt and black pepper.

Meanwhile, cook the pasta in a large saucepan of lightly salted boiling water according to the package directions, until al dente. Drain and return to the pan.

Stir the sauce into the cooked pasta and toss well. Season with freshly ground black pepper and serve immediately with the cheese.

For penne with fennel & basil, heat 3 tablespoons olive oil in a skillet, add 2 crushed garlic cloves and a pinch of dried red pepper flakes and cook, stirring, for 1 minute. Add 1 trimmed and thinly sliced fennel bulb and cook gently for about 10 minutes, until soft and golden. Meanwhile, cook 8 oz fresh penne in a large saucepan of lightly salted boiling water according to the package directions, until al dente. Drain, reserving 2 tablespoons of the cooking water, and return to the pan. Add the fennel mixture and the reserved cooking water and stir well, then toss in 1 tablespoon shredded basil leaves. Serve immediately, sprinkled with 2 tablespoons grated vegetarian Parmesan-style cheese.

spinach & potato gratin

Serves **4**
Preparation time **10 minutes**
Cooking time **35 minutes**

5 **white round** or **red-skinned**
   potatoes, peeled and
   thinly sliced
1 lb **spinach leaves**
1¾ cups shredded
   mozzarella cheese
4 **tomatoes**, sliced
3 **eggs**, beaten
1¼ cups **heavy cream**
salt and **black pepper**

Cook the potatoes in a large saucepan of salted boiling water for 5 minutes, then drain well.

Meanwhile, cook the spinach in a separate saucepan of boiling water for 1–2 minutes. Drain and squeeze out the excess water.

Grease a large ovenproof dish and line the bottom with half the potato slices. Cover with the spinach and half the mozzarella, seasoning each layer well with salt and black pepper. Cover with the remaining potato slices and arrange the tomato slices on top. Sprinkle with the remaining mozzarella.

Beat together the eggs and cream in a bowl and season well with salt and black pepper. Pour the sauce over the ingredients in the dish.

Bake in a preheated oven, at 350°F, for about 30 minutes. Serve immediately.

For tomato, lime & basil salad, to serve as an accompaniment, slice or quarter 8 tomatoes while the gratin is baking, then arrange in a large serving bowl. Sprinkle with ½ red onion, thinly sliced, and a handful of basil leaves. Whisk together ¼ cup olive oil, 2 tablespoons chopped basil, 1 tablespoon lime juice, 1 teaspoon grated lime zest, ½ teaspoon honey, 1 crushed garlic clove, a pinch of cayenne pepper, and salt and black pepper to taste. Pour the dressing over the salad. Cover and let stand at room temperature for about 30 minutes to let the flavors mingle, then serve with the gratin.

mexican bean burgers

Serves 4
Preparation time **15 minutes**,
    plus cooling
Cooking time **12–15 minutes**

1 tablespoon **sunflower oil**
1 **onion**, finely chopped
1 **green chile**, seeded and
    finely chopped
2 teaspoons **Mexican** or **fajita
    spice mix**
2 (15 oz) cans **red kidney
    beans**, drained and rinsed
2 cups **fresh white bread
    crumbs**
¼ cup chopped **fresh cilantro**
1 **egg**
2 teaspoons **chipotle paste**
salt and **black pepper**

To serve
4 **burger buns**
crisp green lettuce
prepared fresh tomato salsa
prepared guacamole

Heat the oil in a small skillet, add the onion and chile, and cook over medium heat for 2–3 minutes until softened. Stir in the spice mix and cook, stirring, for 1 minute. Let cool slightly.

Mash the beans in a large bowl with a potato masher or fork, then add the bread crumbs and cilantro and season well with salt and black pepper.

Beat the egg with the paste in a small bowl, then add to the bean mixture and mix together well with a fork.

Divide the bean mixture into 4 and shape each portion into a patty.

Place the patties on a nonstick baking sheet and cook under a preheated medium-high broiler for 4–5 minutes on each side, until golden and cooked through.

Slice the buns in half horizontally. Top the bottom halves of the buns with some lettuce and a spoonful of salsa. Place the burgers on top and finish with a spoonful of guacamole. Cover with the top halves of the buns.

For spicy Mexican meatballs, prepare the bean mixture as above, then shape into 16–18 balls. Heat 1 tablespoon sunflower oil in a large skillet, add the meatballs, and cook for 4–5 minutes, turning occasionally. Pour over 2 cups tomato puree or tomato sauce and add 1 teaspoon each of dried oregano and granulated sugar. Cover and simmer for 10 minutes. Serve with rice and a spoonful of sour cream.

golden mushroom & leek pies

Serves **4**
Preparation time **15 minutes**
Cooking time **25–30 minutes**

2 tablespoons **butter**
2 **leeks**, trimmed, cleaned, and
   thinly sliced
5 cups trimmed, quartered
   cremini mushrooms
4¼ cups trimmed, quartered
   button mushrooms
1 tablespoon **all-purpose
   flour**
1 cup **milk**
⅔ cup **heavy cream**
1 cup shredded **sharp
   cheddar cheese**
¼ cup finely chopped **parsley**
2 sheets of **store-bought puff
   pastry**, defrosted if frozen
beaten egg, to glaze

Melt the butter in a large saucepan, add the leeks, and cook over medium heat for 1–2 minutes. Add the mushrooms and cook for 2 minutes.

Stir in the flour and cook, stirring, for 1 minute, then gradually add the milk and cream and cook, stirring constantly, until the sauce boils and thickens. Add the cheddar and parsley and cook, stirring, for 1–2 minutes. Remove from the heat.

Cut 4 circles from the pastry sheets to cover 4 individual pie dishes. Divide the mushroom mixture among the pie dishes. Brush the rims with the beaten egg, then place the pastry circles on top. Press down around the rims and crimp the edges with a fork. Cut a couple of slits in the top of each pie to let the steam out. Brush the pastry with the remaining beaten egg.

Bake in a preheated oven, at 425°F, for 15–20 minutes, until the pastry is golden brown. Serve hot.

spiced tofu, noodles & bok choy

Serves **4**
Preparation time **10 minutes**,
 plus standing
Cooking time **10 minutes**

10 oz **firm tofu**, drained
8 oz **dried medium
 egg noodles**
1 tablespoon **cornstarch**
½ teaspoon **salt**
1 teaspoon **ground
 black pepper**
½ teaspoon **Chinese five-
 spice powder**
2 tablespoons **sunflower oil**
1 inch piece of **fresh ginger
 root**, peeled and finely
 chopped
1 tablespoon **dark soy sauce**
2 tablespoons **sweet
 chili sauce**
½ cup **water**
2 heads of **bok choy**, trimmed
 and leaves separated to
 the pan

Place the tofu between 2 pieces of paper towels and set a cutting board or other weight on top. Let stand for at least 10 minutes to remove excess water.

Remove the weight and paper towels, then cut the tofu into cubes.

Cook the noodles according to the package directions. Drain and set aside.

Mix together the cornstarch, salt, black pepper, and five-spice powder in a bowl and use to coat the tofu. Heat 1 tablespoon of the oil in a wok or large skillet over high heat. Add the tofu and stir-fry for 2–3 minutes, until golden. Remove from the pan and keep warm.

Heat the remaining oil in the pan, add the ginger, and stir-fry for 1 minute. Add the noodles, stir in the soy sauce, chili sauce, and measured water, then add the bok choy. Cook, stirring, until the leaves start to wilt.

Divide the noodles among plates and top with the tofu.

For stir-fried tofu with hoisin sauce, prepare and stir-fry the tofu as above, omitting the coating. Remove from the pan and keep warm. Add 1 crushed garlic clove and 2 teaspoons chopped fresh ginger to the pan and stir-fry for 1 minute. Add 8 oz trimmed baby broccoli, 2 cups halved snow peas, and 1 bunch of scallions, chopped, and stir-fry for 2–3 minutes, then stir in ¼ cup toasted cashew nuts, 2 tablespoons hoisin sauce, 2 tablespoons water, and 1 tablespoon soy sauce. Return the tofu to the pan and simmer for 1 minute to heat through.

mushroom & spinach lasagne

Serves **4**
Preparation time **15 minutes**
Cooking time **10 minutes**

3 tablespoons **extra virgin olive oil**
1 lb **mixed mushrooms**, trimmed and sliced
1 cup **mascarpone cheese**
12 **fresh lasagna noodles**
5 oz **Taleggio cheese**, rind removed and cut into cubes
4 cups **baby spinach leaves**
salt and **black pepper**

Heat the oil in a large skillet, add the mushrooms, and cook over medium heat for 5 minutes. Add the mascarpone and cook over high heat for 1 minute, until thickened. Season to taste with salt and black pepper.

Meanwhile, put the pasta noodles in a large roasting pan and cover with boiling water. Let stand for about 5 minutes, until tender, then drain.

Brush an ovenproof dish lightly with oil and place 3 pasta noodles over the bottom, slightly overlapping. Top the pasta with a little of the Taleggio, one-third of the mushroom sauce, and one-third of the spinach. Repeat the process with 2 more layers, then top the final layer of pasta with the remaining Taleggio.

Place the dish under a preheated high broiler and cook for 5 minutes, until the cheese is golden brown. Serve immediately.

For mushroom, tomato & zucchini lasagne, use 4 tomatoes and 2 zucchini in place of the spinach. Blanch the tomatoes in a saucepan of boiling water, then skin and slice, and thinly slice the zucchini, before proceeding with the recipe, as above.

root vegetable & bean gratin

Serves **4–6**
Preparation time **20 minutes**
Cooking time **50–55 minutes**

1 tablespoon **olive oil**
2 **carrots**, sliced
2 **parsnips**, peeled and
  chopped
2 **leeks**, trimmed, cleaned
  and sliced
1¼ cups **red wine**
1 (14½ oz) can **diced
  tomatoes**
1¼ cup **vegetable stock**
1 (15 oz) can **lima beans**,
  drained and rinsed
1 tablespoon chopped
  rosemary
salt and **black pepper**

Crumble topping
3½ slices **whole-wheat
  bread**, coarsely torn
  into pieces
½ cup coarsely chopped
  walnuts
2 tablespoons chopped
  flat leaf parsley
1 cup shredded **Monterey
  Jack** or **cheddar cheese**

Heat the oil in a large saucepan, add the carrots, parsnips, and leeks, and cook over medium heat for 4–5 minutes, until slightly softened.

Stir the wine into the pan and cook until reduced by half, then stir in the tomatoes, stock, lima beans, and rosemary. Season well with salt and black pepper, then cover and simmer for 15 minutes, stirring occasionally. Transfer to a 2 quart ovenproof dish.

Meanwhile, make the crumble topping. Put the bread, walnuts, parsley, and ¾ cup of the cheese into a food processor and pulse until the mixture resembles bread crumbs.

Spoon the topping over the vegetable mixture and sprinkle with the remaining cheese. Bake in a preheated oven, at 350°F, for 25–30 minutes, until golden and crisp. Serve immediately with steamed green vegetables, if liked.

For lima bean & root vegetable pie, prepare the root vegetable filling as above and place in the ovenproof dish. Spoon 4–5 cups warmed, prepared mashed potatoes over the top of the vegetable mixture. Sprinkle with 1 cup shredded sharp cheddar cheese and bake as above for 15–20 minutes, until the topping is golden.

spring vegetable & herb pilaf

Serves **4**
Preparation time **15 minutes**
Cooking time **20 minutes**

2 tablespoons **extra virgin olive oil**
1 **leek**, trimmed, cleaned and sliced
1 **zucchini**, diced
grated zest and juice of 1 **lemon**
2 **garlic cloves**, crushed
1⅔ cups **white long-grain rice**
2½ cups **hot vegetable stock**
1½ cup chopped **green beans**
1 cup **fresh** or **frozen peas**
¼ cup chopped **mixed herbs**, such as mint, parsley and chives
½ cup **slivered almonds**, toasted
salt and **black pepper**

Heat the olive oil in a large skillet, add the leek, zucchini, lemon zest, garlic, and a little salt and black pepper, and cook gently for 5 minutes.

Add the rice, stir once, and pour in the hot stock. Bring to a boil, then reduce the heat, cover, and simmer gently according to the package directions for the rice.

Stir in the beans and peas in the final 5 minutes, replacing the lid.

Remove the pan from the heat and let stand for 5 minutes. Stir in the lemon juice and herbs and serve sprinkled with the slivered almonds.

For winter vegetable & fruit pilaf, heat 2 tablespoons extra virgin olive oil in a large skillet, add 1 sliced red onion, 1 teaspoon ground coriander, and 2 teaspoons chopped thyme, and cook gently for 5 minutes. Add 3 cups diced butternut squash pumpkin flesh with the rice as above, stir once, and pour in the hot stock. Bring to a boil, then reduce the heat, cover, and simmer gently according to the package directions on the rice. Stir in ½ cup raisins with the peas as above, cover, and cook for the final 5 minutes. Remove the pan from the heat and let stand for 5 minutes. Stir in 2 tablespoons chopped fresh cilantro with the lemon juice and almonds.

macaroni & cheese with spinach

Serves **4**
Preparation time **10 minutes**
Cooking time **30 minutes**

10 oz **dried macaroni**
1 (12 oz) package **baby
  spinach leaves**
4 tablespoons **butter**
⅓ cup **all-purpose flour**
3 cups **milk**
1 cup diced **Taleggio** or
  fontina cheese
2 teaspoons **whole-grain
  mustard**
1 teaspoon **Dijon mustard**
8 **cherry tomatoes**, halved
1 cup **fresh white bread
  crumbs**
¼ cup shredded **cheddar
  cheese**
salt and **black pepper**

Cook the macaroni in a large saucepan of lightly salted boiling water according to the package directions, until al dente.

Add the spinach to the pan and cook for 1 minute until wilted. Drain well and transfer to a 1½ quart ovenproof dish.

Meanwhile, put the butter, flour, and milk into a saucepan and whisk constantly over medium heat until the sauce boils and thickens. Simmer for 2–3 minutes, until you have a smooth glossy sauce, then reduce the heat to low and stir in the Taleggio or fontina and mustards. Season to taste with salt and black pepper and cook gently until the cheese has melted.

Pour the sauce over the macaroni and spinach, sprinkle with the tomatoes, and then sprinkle with the bread crumbs and cheddar.

Bake in a preheated oven, at 400°F, for 20 minutes, until golden and bubbling.

For macaroni & cheese with broccoli & cauliflower, cook the macaroni as above, steaming 4 cups small broccoli and cauliflower florets above the pan for 5 minutes, until tender. Drain the pasta and vegetables well and transfer to a 1½ quart ovenproof dish. Make the cheese sauce as above and pour over the macaroni and vegetables. Sprinkle with the bread crumbs and cheddar and bake as above until golden and bubbling.

spicy goan eggplant curry

Serves **4**
Preparation time **15 minutes**
Cooking time about
  25 minutes

4 teaspoons **coriander seeds**
1 teaspoon **cumin seeds**
1 teaspoon **cayenne pepper**
2 **green chile**, seeded
  and sliced
½ teaspoon **ground turmeric**
4 **garlic cloves**, crushed
1 tablespoon peeled and
  grated **fresh ginger root**
1¼ cups **warm water**
1¾ cups **coconut milk**
1 tablespoon **tamarind paste**
1 large **eggplant**, thinly sliced
  lengthwise
salt and **black pepper**
pita or **naan bread**, to serve

Toast the coriander and cumin seeds in a dry skillet over medium heat until aromatic, then crush lightly with a mortar and pestle.

Put the crushed spices into a large saucepan with the cayenne, chile, turmeric, garlic, ginger, and the measured water. Bring to a boil, then reduce the heat and simmer for 10 minutes, until thickened. Season to taste with salt and black pepper and stir in the coconut milk and tamarind paste.

Arrange the eggplant slices in a broiler pan lined with aluminum foil and brush the tops with some of the curry sauce. Cook under a preheated high broiler, turning once, until golden and tender.

Serve the eggplant slices in the curry sauce with naan or pita bread.

For cashew & zucchini curry, prepare the curry sauce as above and add 2 cups toasted cashew nuts to the finished sauce. To toast, soak in water for 20 minutes, then drain and chop. Heat in a dry skillet over medium heat, shaking frequently, until lightly browned. Continue with the recipe as above, using 4 sliced zucchini in place of the eggplant. Drizzle the finished dish with walnut oil and season with salt and black pepper.

asparagus, mint & lemon risotto

Serves **4**
Preparation time **10 minutes**
Cooking time **25–30 minutes**

1 lb **asparagus spears**,
  woody ends removed
1 **vegetable bouillon cube**
2 tablespoons **butter**
1 tablespoon **olive oil**
1 **onion**, chopped
1 ½ cups **risotto rice**
⅔ cup **dry white wine**
grated zest and juice of
  1 lemon
¼ cup chopped **mint**
½ cup grated **vegetarian
  Parmesan-style cheese**,
  plus extra to serve

Chop the asparagus stems finely, leaving the tips whole. Cook the asparagus tips and stems in a saucepan of simmering water for about 3 minutes, until al dente. Drain, reserving the cooking water.

Pour the reserved cooking water over the bouillon cube in a liquid measuring cup, making it up to 4 cups with boiling water and stir to dissolve the cube.

Meanwhile, melt the butter with the oil in a saucepan, add the onion, and cook over medium heat for about 2 minutes, until softened. Stir in the rice and cook for 1 minute, stirring, until well coated in the onion mixture.

Pour in the wine and cook for 2–3 minutes, until absorbed. Gradually add the hot stock, ½ cup at a time, stirring constantly and cooking until most of the liquid has been absorbed before adding the next batch of stock. Continue until almost all of the stock has been absorbed and the rice is creamy but still firm. This will take about 15 minutes.

Stir in the asparagus tips and stems and cook for 2–3 minutes, until heated through. Stir in the lemon zest and juice, mint, and cheese. Cover and let stand for about 1 minute. Serve in bowls with extra grated cheese for sprinkling.

For asparagus & goat cheese risotto, follow the recipe above to prepare the risotto, omitting the mint and cheese and stirring 4 oz chopped creamy goat cheese and 2 tablespoons chopped parsley into the cooked risotto. Cover and let stand for about 1 minute before serving.

zucchini & creamy tomato penne

Serves **4**

Preparation time **10 minutes**

Cooking time **12 minutes**

1 tablespoon **olive oil**

1 **onion**, chopped

1 **garlic clove**, finely chopped

3 **zucchini**, chopped

1 **red bell pepper**, cored,
  seeded, and chopped

¾ cup **mascarpone cheese**

1 cup **tomato puree** or
  tomato sauce

2 tablespoons chopped **basil**

1 lb **fresh penne**

salt and **black pepper**

Heat the oil in a skillet, add the onion and garlic, and cook over medium heat for 3 minutes, until softened. Stir in the zucchini and red bell pepper and cook for 5 minutes, until the zucchini have softened.

Stir the mascarpone into the pan until melted, then add the tomato puree or sauce and simmer for 2–3 minutes. Season to taste with salt and black pepper and stir in the basil.

Meanwhile, cook the pasta in a large saucepan of lightly salted boiling water according to the package directions, until al dente. Drain and return to the pan.

Stir the sauce into the cooked pasta and toss well. Serve immediately with the basil sprinkled over the top.

For gnocchi with creamy tomato sauce, cook 1 lb fresh gnocchi in a large saucepan of boiling water according to the package directions, until they rise to the surface, then drain. Meanwhile, gently heat the tomato puree or tomato sauce in a saucepan and stir in the mascarpone cheese until melted. Simmer for 2–3 minutes, then stir in 1 (7 oz) package baby spinach leaves until wilted. Stir the cooked gnocchi into the sauce, season with black pepper, and serve immediately with grated vegetarian Parmesan-style cheese.

leek & chestnut patties

Serves **4**
Preparation time **20 minutes**
Cooking time **15 minutes**

2 **rutabagas**, peeled and diced
3–4 tablespoons **low-fat milk**
4 **leeks**, trimmed, cleaned, and
 finely chopped
5 **soft pitted prunes**, finely
 chopped
½ cup coarsely chopped
 Brazil nuts
20 canned **whole peeled**
 chestnuts, crumbled
2½ cups **fresh white**
 bread crumbs
1 **egg**, lightly beaten
3 tablespoons **sunflower oil**
salt and **black pepper**
parsley sprigs, to garnish

Cranberry sauce
2 teaspoons **cornstarch**
1 cup **vegetable stock**
2 tablespoons **cranberry**
 sauce
1 tablespoon **red wine vinegar**
1 teaspoon **Dijon mustard**
1 teaspoon **tomato paste**

Cook the rutabagas in a saucepan of boiling water for 15 minutes, until tender. Drain and return to the pan. Mash with the milk, season to taste with salt and black pepper, and keep warm.

Meanwhile, mix together the leeks, prunes, Brazil nuts, and chestnuts in a large bowl. Mix in the bread crumbs, egg, and salt and black pepper. Shape the mixture into 16 patties with lightly floured hands.

Heat the oil in a skillet, add the patties, and cook over medium heat for 10 minutes, turning several times, until browned and heated through.

Make the sauce. Mix the cornstarch with a little water in a small bowl until smooth. Put the remaining sauce ingredients into a small bowl, add the cornstarch mixture, and stir.

Push the patties to one side of the pan, add the sauce mixture, and bring to a boil, stirring constantly, until thickened.

Spoon the mashed rutabagas onto warmed plates and top with the patties and sauce. Garnish with the parsley and serve.

tikka lentil koftas

Serves **4**

Preparation time **20 minutes**

Cooking time **12–15 minutes**

3 tablespoons **sunflower oil**

1 **onion**, finely chopped

1 **garlic clove**, crushed

1 teaspoon peeled and
chopped **fresh ginger root**

1 **green chile**, seeded and
finely chopped

2 tablespoons **tikka curry
paste**

grated zest and juice of
½ **lemon**

2 (15 oz) cans **green lentils**,
drained and rinsed, or 2 cups
dried green lentils, cooked

2 tablespoons chopped
fresh cilantro

½ cup **fresh white
bread crumbs**

all-purpose flour, for coating

1 extra-large **egg**, lightly
beaten

¾ cup **dried natural
bread crumbs**

salt and **black pepper**

To serve

cucumber and mint yogurt

green salad leaves

Heat 1 tablespoon of the oil in a large saucepan,
add the onion, garlic, ginger, and chile, and cook over
medium heat for 3–4 minutes, until softened. Stir in the
curry paste and lemon zest and juice and cook, stirring,
for 1 minute.

Remove the pan from the heat and stir in the lentils,
cilantro, and fresh bread crumbs, then season well with
salt and black pepper. Mix well, mashing with a spoon so
that the mixture holds together.

Divide the mixture into 8 equal portions, using slightly
wet hands. Flatten slightly, then roll in the flour. Place
the beaten egg and dried bread crumbs in separate
dishes. Dip each kofta in the egg and then in the bread
crumbs until coated.

Heat the remaining oil in a large saucepan, add the
koftas, and cook over medium heat for 4–5 minutes on
each side, until crisp and golden. Serve with cucumber
and mint yogurt and a crisp green salad.

For lentil & spinach tikka, cook the onion, garlic,
ginger, and chile as above, then stir in the curry paste
and lemon zest and juice and cook, stirring, for 1 minute.
Add the lentils with 1 (14½ oz) can diced tomatoes and
⅔ cup vegetable stock. Simmer for 10–15 minutes, until
thickened. Stir in 8 cups baby spinach leaves and cook
until just wilted. Stir in 2 tablespoons chopped fresh
cilantro and serve hot with naan or pita bread.

orecchiette with walnut sauce

Serves **4**
Preparation time **5 minutes**
Cooking time **11–13 minutes**

12 oz **dried orecchiette**
4 tablespoons **butter**
15 **sage leaves**, coarsely chopped
2 **garlic cloves**, finely chopped
1 cup finely chopped **walnuts**
⅔ cup **light cream**
¾ cup **vegetarian Parmesan-style cheese**, freshly grated
salt and **black pepper**

Cook the pasta in a large saucepan of lightly salted boiling water according to the package directions, until al dente.

Meanwhile, melt the butter in a skillet over medium heat. When it begins to foam and sizzle, stir in the sage and garlic and cook, stirring, for 1–2 minutes, until golden. Remove from the heat and stir in the walnuts, cream, and cheese.

Drain the pasta and stir it thoroughly into the sauce. Season to taste with salt and black pepper and serve immediately.

For spinach, scallion & avocado salad, to serve as an accompaniment, put 5 cups baby spinach leaves, 4 finely sliced scallions, and 2 pitted, peeled, and sliced avocados in a large bowl and toss together. Spoon into separate side dishes.

oven-baked squash with quinoa

Serves **4**
Preparation time **10 minutes**
Cooking time **40 minutes**

2 tablespoons **olive oil**
1 **butternut squash**,
  peeled, seeded, and cut
  into 1½ inch chunks
2 tablespoons **unsalted
  butter**
1 **red onion**, chopped
1 **garlic clove**, crushed
⅓ cup **pine nuts**
2 cups **quinoa**
⅔ cup **dry white wine**
1 **cinnamon stick**
4 cups **vegetable stock**
¼ cup chopped **mint**
1⅓ cups crumbled **feta
  cheese**
½ cup **pomegranate seeds**
salt and **black pepper**

Heat the oil in a large skillet and add the squash in a single layer. Season well with salt and black pepper and cook over medium heat for about 10 minutes, until lightly browned.

Meanwhile, melt the butter in a flameproof casserole dish, add the onion and garlic, and cook for 2–3 minutes, until softened. Stir in the pine nuts and quinoa and cook for 1 minute or until the quinoa is starting to pop. Add the wine and cook until it has been absorbed.

Stir in the squash, cinnamon stick, and stock. Bring to a boil, season to taste with salt and black pepper, and stir well.

Cover the dish with the lid and cook in a preheated oven, at 375°F, for 25 minutes, until the quinoa is just tender.

Stir in the mint, then sprinkle with the feta and pomegranate seeds. Serve immediately.

asian mushroom packages

Makes **4**
Preparation time **25 minutes**
Cooking time **25 minutes**

4 large **portobello mushrooms**
1 tablespoon **sesame oil**
1 tablespoon **kecap manis** or **soy sauce**
1 inch piece of **fresh ginger root**, peeled and finely chopped
2 **garlic cloves**, finely chopped
¼ cup coarsely chopped **fresh cilantro**
1 **tomato**, cut into 4 thick slices
2 tablespoons **butter**, cut into 4 pieces
1 lb **prepared rolled dough pie crust**, defrosted if frozen
beaten egg, to glaze
4 teaspoons **sesame seeds**
black pepper

Trim the top of the mushroom stems level with the caps, drizzle the gills with the sesame oil and kecap manis or soy sauce, and then sprinkle with the ginger, garlic, and cilantro. Top each with a slice of tomato, a piece of butter, and a little black pepper.

Cut the dough into 4 pieces, roll out one piece thinly on a lightly floured surface to a 7–8 inch circle, or large enough to enclose the mushrooms (this will depend on how big they are, so make a little larger, if necessary).

Place a mushroom on top of each dough circle, brush the edges with beaten egg, then lift the dough up and over the top of the mushroom, pleating the dough as you work and pinching the ends together in the center of the mushroom to completely enclose it.

Transfer the packages to a greased baking sheet, brush with beaten egg, and sprinkle with the sesame seeds. Bake in a preheated oven, at 400°F, for about 25 minutes, until golden brown. Serve hot with soy sauce, and stir-fried vegetables, if desired.

For French mushroom packages, drizzle 4 large trimmed portobello mushrooms with 1 tablespoon olive oil and 2 tablespoons red wine, then top with 2 finely chopped garlic cloves, 2 tablespoons each of chopped basil and chives, and 4 slices of goat cheese cut from a 4 oz log. Season to taste with salt and black pepper, then wrap in rolled dough pie crust as above, brush with beaten egg to glaze, and top with a slice of onion. Bake as above.

mixed mushroom spaghetti

Serves **4**

Preparation time **20 minutes,**
plus soaking

Cooking time **1 hour–1 hour
10 minutes**

1 oz **dried wild mushrooms,**
such as porcini and
chanterelle

2 tablespoons **olive oil**

1 large **onion,** chopped

1 **celery stick,** finely chopped

1 **carrot,** finely chopped

2 **garlic cloves,** crushed

1 lb **mixed mushrooms,**
trimmed and coarsely
chopped

⅔ cup **red wine**

1 (14½ oz) can **diced
tomatoes**

1 tablespoon **tomato paste**

1 teaspoon **balsamic vinegar**

2 teaspoons **dried oregano**

12 oz **dried spaghetti**

salt and **black pepper**

grated **vegetarian Parmesan-
style cheese,** to serve

Put the dried mushrooms into a bowl and pour over
enough hot water to cover. Let soak for 20 minutes.

Heat the oil in a large saucepan, add the onion, celery,
carrot, and garlic, and cook over low heat for 8 minutes,
stirring occasionally, until softened. Increase the heat,
stir in the fresh mushrooms, and cook for 3–4 minutes.

Strain the soaked dried mushrooms through a strainer,
reserving the liquid. Add the mushrooms to the pan.

Pour in the wine, bring to a boil, and cook until reduced
by half. Stir in the reserved soaking liquid, tomatoes,
tomato paste, vinegar, and oregano, season with salt
and black pepper, and bring to a boil.

Reduce the heat, cover, and simmer for 40–50 minutes,
until the sauce is thick and the mushrooms are tender.

Meanwhile, cook the spaghetti in a large saucepan
of lightly salted boiling water according to the package
directions, until al dente. Drain and serve immediately
topped with the mushroom mixture, with vegetarian
Parmesan-style pasta cheese grated over.

For mushroom stroganoff, melt 2 tablespoons
unsalted butter in a large skillet, add 1 lb mushrooms,
trimmed and sliced, and 1 crushed garlic clove, and
cook for 5–6 minutes, until the mushrooms are
browned. Stir in 1 teaspoon paprika and 1 tablespoon
brandy and cook for 1 minute. Add 1¼ cups sour
cream and simmer for 1 minute, stir in 2 tablespoons
chopped parsley, and serve with rice.

asparagus & snow pea stir-fry

Serves **4**

Preparation time **10 minutes**

Cooking time **7–10 minutes**

2 tablespoons **vegetable oil**

2½ inch piece of **fresh ginger root**, peeled and thinly shredded

2 large **garlic cloves**, thinly sliced

4 **scallions**, diagonally sliced

8 oz **thin asparagus spears**, cut into 1¼ inch lengths

2½ cups diagonally halved **snow peas**

1½ cups **bean sprouts**

3 tablespoons **light soy sauce**, plus extra to serve (optional)

Heat a large wok or skillet until smoking, add the oil, then add the ginger and garlic. Stir-fry for 30 seconds. Add the scallions and stir-fry for 30 seconds, then add the asparagus and stir-fry for another 3–4 minutes.

Add the snow peas to the pan and stir-fry for 2–3 minutes, until the vegetables are still crunchy but beginning to soften.

Stir in the bean sprouts and toss in the hot oil for 1–2 minutes. Pour in the soy sauce, then serve immediately with steamed rice and extra soy sauce, if desired.

For stir-fried vegetable omelets, follow the recipe above to prepare the stir-fried vegetables and keep warm. For each omelet, beat 3 eggs with 2 tablespoons water and salt and black pepper in a bowl. Heat a little vegetable oil in an omelet pan or small skillet over medium heat, then swirl in one-quarter of the egg mixture. Fork over the omelet so that it cooks evenly. As soon as it is set on the bottom (but still a little runny in the middle), top with one-quarter of the stir-fried vegetables and cook for another 30 seconds. Carefully slide the omelet onto a warmed plate, folding it in half as you do so. Keep warm while you make another 3 omelets in the same way.

savory bread & butter pudding

Serves **4**

Preparation time **15 minutes**,
plus standing

Cooking time **30–35 minutes**

2 tablespoons **butter**,
softened

1 **garlic clove**, crushed

4 thick slices **stale
white bread**

12 **cherry tomatoes**, plus
1 small bunch of **vine
cherry tomatoes**

1 cup shredded **sharp
cheddar cheese**

2 tablespoons chopped **basil**

3 **eggs**

1 teaspoon **smoked paprika**

2 cups **milk**

salt and **black pepper**

Mix together the butter and garlic in a small bowl, then grease the bottom of a shallow 1 quart ovenproof dish with a little of the butter.

Cut the crusts from the bread, then spread each slice with the remaining butter. Cut each slice in half and arrange half the buttered bread in the bottom of the dish. Sprinkle with the 12 tomatoes, half the cheese, and 1 tablespoon of the basil. Arrange the buttered bread on top and sprinkle with the remaining basil.

Whisk together the eggs and paprika in a bowl, then whisk in the milk, season with salt and black pepper, and pour the mixture over the bread. Let stand for 10 minutes, then sprinkle with the remaining cheese and top with the bunch of tomatoes. Bake in a preheated oven, at 350°F, for 30–35 minutes, until golden and just set. Serve hot with a crisp green salad.

For mushroom & thyme bread pudding, heat 1 tablespoon olive oil in a large skillet, add 1 lb mixed mushrooms, trimmed and sliced, 1 teaspoon chopped garlic, and 2 teaspoons chopped thyme. Cook over medium heat for 3–4 minutes, until softened. Prepare the bread as above, arrange half in the bottom of the buttered dish and top with half the mushroom mixture and 2 oz grated hard goat cheese. Repeat with the remaining bread and mushrooms. Whisk the eggs and milk as above, omitting the paprika, season with salt and black pepper, pour the eggs over the bread and mushrooms, and let stand for 10 minutes. Sprinkle with the remaining cheese and bake as above.

braised leek & bell peppers

Serves **4**
Preparation time **5 minutes**
Cooking time **20 minutes**

2 tablespoons **olive oil**
2 **leeks**, trimmed, cleaned
    and cut into ½ inch pieces
1 **orange bell pepper**,
    cored, seeded, and cut
    into ½ inch chunks
1 **red bell pepper**, cored,
    seeded, and cut into
    ½ inch chunks
3 tablespoons **balsamic
    vinegar**
handful of **flat leaf parsley**,
    chopped
salt and **black pepper**

Heat the oil in a saucepan, add the leeks and bell peppers, and stir well. Cover and cook gently for 10 minutes.

Add the vinegar to the pan and cook, uncovered, for another 10 minutes. The vegetables should be brown from the vinegar and all the liquid should have evaporated.

Season well with salt and black pepper, then stir in the chopped parsley just before serving.

For balsamic braised onions, put 1 lb pearl onions, peeled but left whole, in a saucepan with 3 tablespoons each of balsamic vinegar and olive oil, 3 tablespoons packed light brown sugar, 2 tablespoons tomato paste, several thyme sprigs, a handful of golden raisins, and 1¼ cups water. Bring to a boil, then reduce the heat and simmer gently, uncovered, for about 40 minutes, until the onions are tender and the sauce syrupy. Serve warm or cold.

bean & potato moussaka

Serves **4**
Preparation time **10 minutes**,
  plus cooling
Cooking time **55–60 minutes**

6 **white round potatoes**,
  washed
1 tablespoon **olive oil**
1 large **onion**, chopped
1 **garlic clove**, crushed
1 large **carrot**, sliced
1 teaspoon **ground cinnamon**
2 teaspoons **dried mixed
  herbs**
1 (14½ oz) can **diced
  tomatoes**
1 (15 oz) can **red kidney
  beans**, drained and rinsed
1¼ cups **vegetable stock**
salt and **black pepper**

Sauce
4 tablespoons **butter**
⅓ cup **all-purpose flour**
2½ cups **milk**
¾ cup shredded **sharp
  cheddar cheese**
1 **egg**

Cook the potatoes in a large saucepan of boiling water
for about 10 minutes, until just tender. Drain and let
stand until cool enough to handle, then remove the
skins and slice into ¼ inch slices.

Heat the oil in a large saucepan, add the onion and
garlic, and cook gently for 3–4 minutes, until softened.
Add the carrot, cinnamon, and herbs, then stir in the
tomatoes, kidney beans, and stock. Season to taste
with salt and black pepper and bring to a boil, then
reduce the heat and simmer, uncovered, for 15 minutes
until thickened.

Meanwhile, make the sauce. Place the butter, flour, and
milk in a saucepan and whisk constantly over medium
heat until the sauce boils and thickens. Simmer for
2–3 minutes, until you have a smooth glossy sauce.
Stir in the cheese and then remove from the heat.
Let cool slightly, then beat in the egg.

Put half the bean mixture into the bottom of a deep
ovenproof dish and top with a layer of potatoes. Repeat,
finishing with a layer of potatoes. Pour the sauce over
the top and bake in a preheated oven, at 350°F, for
25–30 minutes, until golden brown. Let stand for
5 minutes before serving.

For cheesy bean baked potatoes, scrub 4 russet
potatoes, then bake in a preheated oven, at 400°F, for
about 1 hour, until cooked through. Meanwhile, follow
the recipe above to prepare the bean filling. Halve the
baked potatoes and spoon the bean mixture over them.
Shred a little cheddar cheese over each and serve
them immediately.

beet chili with papaya salsa

Serves **4**
Preparation time **15 minutes**
Cooking time **1 hour 35
  minutes**

1 tablespoon **sunflower oil**
1 **onion**, chopped
2 **garlic cloves**, finely chopped
6 **raw beets**, peeled and cubed
1 (15 oz) can **red kidney
  beans**, drained and rinsed
1–2 teaspoons **dried red
  pepper flakes**, to taste
2 teaspoons **paprika**
1 teaspoon **ground cinnamon**
1 (14½ oz) can **diced tomatoes**
2 cups **vegetable stock**
2 tablespoons **red wine vinegar**
1 tablespoon packed **dark
  brown sugar**
salt and **black pepper**
sour cream and **brown rice**,
  to serve

Salsa
1 **papaya**, peeled, seeded,
  and diced
½ small **red onion**, finely
  chopped
1 **tomato**, seeded and diced
small bunch of fresh cilantro,
  coarsely chopped

Heat the oil in a flameproof casserole, add the onion, and cook over medium heat for 5 minutes, until lightly browned. Stir in the garlic, beet, kidney beans, red pepper flakes, and spices, then add the tomatoes, stock, vinegar, sugar, and plenty of salt and black pepper.

Bring to a boil, then cover and transfer to a preheated oven, at 350°F, for 1½ hours or until the beet is tender.

Meanwhile, make the salsa. Mix all the salsa ingredients together in a bowl, then spoon into a serving dish, cover, and chill in the refrigerator.

Serve the chili in bowls with the brown rice, and topped with spoonfuls of the salsa, along with some sour cream.

For beet, chili & orange salad, follow the recipe above to cook the beet chili and let cool completely, then stir in the grated zest and juice of 1 orange. Spoon onto lettuce leaves, top with low-fat plain yogurt sprinkled with mint leaves, and garnish with orange segments.

soups
& stews

singapore noodle soup

Serves **4**

Preparation time **5 minutes**,
plus standing

Cooking time **5 minutes**

8 oz **dried flat rice noodles**

1 tablespoon **Singapore
noodle paste**

1 cup **green beans**

1 **carrot**, cut into thin strips

1¾ cups **coconut milk**

3 cups **hot vegetable stock**

1 cup **bean sprouts**

1 (8 oz) can **bamboo shoots**,
drained

2 tablespoons chopped **fresh
cilantro**

To serve

4 **scallions**, thinly sliced

1 small **red chile**, thinly sliced
(optional)

Prepare the noodles according to the package
directions, until just tender.

Meanwhile, place the Singapore noodle paste in
a large saucepan, add the beans and carrot, and stir
together thoroughly until the vegetables are coated
in the spice mix. Cook, stirring, over medium heat
for 1–2 minutes.

Stir the coconut milk and hot stock into the pan, then
add the bean sprouts and bamboo shoots and simmer
for 3 minutes. Stir in the cilantro.

Drain the noodles, divide among 4 warmed, large, deep
bowls and ladle the soup over the noodles.

Top with the scallions and chile, if using, and serve
immediately with lime wedges.

For miso noodle & mushroom soup, dissolve
4 (⅓ oz) envelopes miso soup mix in 4 cups boiling
water in a saucepan. Add 2 teaspoons peeled and
chopped fresh ginger root and 5 oz each baby broccoli
tips and shiitake mushrooms, trimmed and sliced. Cover
and simmer for 4–5 minutes, until the vegetables are
tender. Stir in 4 oz dried rice noodles. Cook according to
the package directions for the noodles, until just tender.
Serve immediately in warmed bowls.

apple & leek soup

Serves **4**
Preparation time **10 minutes**
Cooking time **25 minutes**

2 tablespoons **butter**
1 tablespoon **sunflower oil**
1 lb **leeks**, trimmed, cleaned,
　and sliced
2 **Yukon gold** or **white round**
　potatoes, peeled and diced
2 **crisp, sweet apples**, peeled,
　cored, and diced
⅔ cup **dry hard cider** or
　apple juice
3¾ cups **vegetable stock**
salt and **black pepper**
shredded **Gruyère cheese**,
　to serve

Melt the butter with the oil in a large saucepan over medium heat, add the leeks, and cook for 5 minutes, until starting to soften.

Stir the potatoes and apples into the pan, cover, and cook for another 5 minutes.

Add the cider or juice and cook, uncovered, until reduced by half. Stir in the stock, cover, and simmer for 15 minutes, until the potatoes are tender.

Serve topped with shredded Gruyère cheese.

For leek & white bean soup, heat 2 tablespoons olive oil in a large saucepan, add 1 lb leeks, trimmed, cleaned, and sliced, and cook for 5 minutes, until softened. Stir in 3 Yukon gold or white round potatoes, peeled and diced, 1 (15 oz) can cannellini beans, drained and rinsed, and 4 cups hot vegetable stock. Bring to a boil, then cover and simmer for 20 minutes, until the vegetables are tender. Stir in 2 tablespoons chopped parsley and serve immediately with freshly ground black pepper.

summer vegetable pistou

Serves **4**
Preparation time **15 minutes**
Cooking time **30 minutes**

2 tablespoons **olive oil**
1 **onion**, chopped
2 **garlic cloves**, crushed
2½ cups **vegetable stock**
8 oz **new potatoes**, scrubbed
  and halved
8 oz **baby carrots**
7 oz **baby zucchini**, halved
  lengthwise
4 **tomatoes**, skinned
  and chopped
1⅓ cups **fresh peas**
salt and **black pepper**
¼ cup **fresh pesto sauce**
  (see right for homemade),
  to serve

Heat the oil in a large saucepan, add the onion and garlic, and cook for 2–3 minutes, until softened.

Pour in the stock, bring to a boil, and add the potatoes. Cover, reduce the heat, and simmer for 10 minutes.

Add the carrots, zucchini, and tomatoes, replace the lid, and simmer for another 10 minutes. Stir in the peas and cook for 4–5 minutes or until all the vegetables are tender. Season to taste with salt and black pepper.

Ladle the soup into large warmed bowls and serve each topped with a tablespoon of pesto, along with crusty bread rolls, if desired.

For homemade fresh pesto sauce, put 2 crushed garlic cloves into a food processor with 3 cups basil leaves and 3 tablespoons pine nuts and blend until the mixture forms a paste. Add 3 tablespoons grated vegetarian Parmesan-style cheese and then, with the motor running, gradually pour in ½ cup olive oil through the feed tube in a thin steady stream until smooth. Season to taste with salt and black pepper.

curried parsnip soup

Serves **4**
Preparation time **15 minutes**
Cooking time **30–35 minutes**

2 tablespoons **butter**
1 tablespoon **sunflower oil**
1 **onion**, chopped
2 **garlic cloves**, crushed
1 inch piece of **fresh ginger root**, peeled and chopped
1 tablespoon **medium curry powder**
1 teaspoon **cumin seeds**
6 **parsnips**, peeled and chopped
salt and **black pepper**

To serve
plain yogurt
2 tablespoons chopped **fresh cilantro**
naan or **pita bread**

Melt the butter with the oil in a large saucepan, add the onion, garlic, and ginger, and cook over medium heat for 4–5 minutes, until softened.

Stir in the curry powder and cumin seeds and cook, stirring, for 2 minutes, then stir in the parsnips, making sure that they are well coated in the spice mixture.

Pour in the stock and bring to a boil, then cover and simmer for 20–25 minutes, until the parsnips are tender. Season to taste with salt and black pepper.

Blend the soup with an immersion blender until smooth, or transfer to a food processor or blender, in batches, to blend. Reheat gently if necessary.

Serve in cups with dollops of plain yogurt, garnished with the cilantro, with the naan or pita bread.

For caramelized parsnip & honey soup, melt 2 tablespoons unsalted butter in a flameproof roasting pan on the stove, add 6 parsnips, peeled and chopped, and 2 thyme sprigs, and turn to coat in the butter. Roast in a preheated oven, at 400° F, for 30–35 minutes, stirring once, until golden brown. Stir in 2 tablespoons honey and roast for another 10 minutes, until the parsnips have caramelized. Transfer to a saucepan, stir in 4 cups vegetable stock, and bring to a boil on the stove, then simmer for 10 minutes. Transfer to a food processor or blender, in batches, and blend until smooth. Return to the pan, season to taste with salt and black pepper, and stir in 1 ¼ cups boiling water, then bring back to a boil. Stir in ¼ cup heavy cream and gently heat through. Serve in bowls with crusty bread.

beet & horseradish soup

Serves **4**
Preparation time **15 minutes**
Cooking time **35 minutes**

1 tablespoon **sunflower oil**
1 **red onion**, chopped
1 **celery stick**, chopped
1 teaspoon **chopped thyme**
6 **raw beets**, peeled and cut
   into small chunks
1 tablespoon **red wine**
   vinegar
3¾ cups hot **vegetable stock**
2 tablespoons **creamed**
   horseradish sauce, plus
   2 teaspoons to serve
3 tablespoons **sour cream**
   or **crème fraîche**
salt and **black pepper**
chopped **chives**, to garnish
crusty bread, to serve

Heat the oil in a large saucepan, add the onion, celery, and thyme, and cook gently for 3–4 minutes. Add the beets and vinegar and cook for 2 minutes.

Pour in the stock, cover, and simmer for 25–30 minutes, until the beets are tender. Season to taste with salt and black pepper and stir in the horseradish sauce.

Blend the soup with an immersion blender until smooth, or transfer to a food processor or blender, in batches, to blend. Reheat gently if necessary.

Mix the sour cream or crème fraîche with the remaining horseradish sauce. Spoon on top of the soup and garnish with chopped chives. Serve with crusty bread.

For beet & caraway soup, heat 1 tablespoon sunflower oil in a large saucepan, add 1 chopped onion and 1 crushed garlic clove, and cook gently for 3–4 minutes, until softened. Stir in 1 teaspoon caraway seeds, 6 raw beets, peeled and diced, 1 potato, peeled and diced, 1 tablespoon cider vinegar, and 3¾ cups vegetable stock. Cover and simmer for 30 minutes, until the beets and potato are tender. Season to taste with salt and black pepper, then blend with an immersion blender until smooth, or transfer to a food processor or blender, in batches, to blend. Reheat gently if necessary. Serve topped with a spoonful of Greek yogurt and a sprinkling of caraway seeds.

potato & smoked garlic soup

Serves **4**
Preparation time **10–15
 minutes**
Cooking time **30–35 minutes**

4 tablespoons **unsalted
 butter**
1 large **onion**, sliced
2 **smoked garlic cloves**,
 crushed
6 **Yukon gold** or **white round
 potatoes**, peeled and cut
 into small cubes
4 cups **vegetable stock**
½ teaspoon **smoked sea salt**
½ cup **milk**
¼ cup **fresh herbs**, such as
 parsley, thyme, and chives,
 plus extra chives to garnish
black pepper
Greek yogurt, to serve

Melt the butter in a large saucepan, add the onion
and smoked garlic, and cook over medium heat for
3–4 minutes, until softened. Stir in the potatoes, cover,
and cook for 5 minutes.

Add the stock and season with the smoked sea salt
and black pepper. Bring to a boil, then reduce the heat,
cover, and simmer for 30 minutes, until the potatoes
are tender.

Transfer to a food processor or blender, in batches, and
blend until smooth. Return to the pan, stir in the milk
and herbs, and reheat gently.

Serve in warmed bowls with a spoonful of Greek
yogurt, garnished with chives and freshly ground
black pepper.

For smoked sweet potato soup, cook the onion and
garlic as above, then add 1 tablespoon smoked paprika
and cook, stirring, for 1 minute. Stir in 3 Yukon gold
or white round potatoes and 3 sweet potatoes, both
peeled and cut into small cubes, and cook for 5 minutes.
Add the stock as above and bring to a boil, then cover
and simmer for 30 minutes, until the potatoes are
tender. Blend as above until smooth, then serve with
a spoonful of Greek yogurt, garnished with a sprinkling
of smoked paprika and freshly snipped chives.

lima bean & vegetable soup

Serves **4**
Preparation time **10 minutes**
Cooking time **25 minutes**

1 tablespoon **olive oil**
2 teaspoons **smoked paprika**
1 **celery stick**, sliced
2 **carrots**, sliced
1 **leek**, trimmed, cleaned,
  and sliced
2½ cups **vegetable stock**
1 (14½ oz) can **diced
  tomatoes**
1 (15 oz) can **lima beans**,
  drained and rinsed
2 teaspoons chopped
  rosemary
salt and **black pepper**
½ cup grated **vegetarian
  Parmesan-style cheese**,
  to serve

Heat the oil in a large saucepan, add the paprika, celery, carrots, and leek, and cook over medium heat for 3–4 minutes, until the vegetables are slightly softened.

Pour in the stock and tomatoes and add the lima beans and rosemary. Season to taste with salt and black pepper and bring to a boil, then cover and simmer for 15 minutes or until the vegetables are just tender.

Ladle into warmed bowls and sprinkle with the cheese and freshly ground black pepper.

For minestrone soup, soften the vegetables in the oil as above, then add the stock, tomatoes, and rosemary with 1 (15 oz) can cranberry beans, drained and rinsed, in place of the lima beans, and simmer for 10 minutes. Add 4 oz dried spaghetti, broken into small pieces, and 1⅓ cups shredded green cabbage and simmer for another 8 minutes, or until the pasta is tender, stirring occasionally. Serve in warmed bowls, sprinkled with the grated vegetarian Parmesan-style cheese as above.

lemon grass & sweet potato curry

Serves **4**
Preparation time **15 minutes**
Cooking time **20 minutes**

2 **lemon grass stalks**
1¾ cups **coconut milk**
⅔ cup **vegetable stock**
1 **garlic clove**, crushed
1 inch piece of **fresh ginger root**, peeled and finely chopped
1 **red chile**, seeded and chopped
2 teaspoons **palm sugar** or **light brown sugar**
6 **kaffir lime leaves**
2 **sweet potatoes**, peeled and chopped
1 **red bell pepper**, cored, seeded, and chopped
1 (6 oz) package **baby spinach leaves**
2 tablespoons **lime juice**
handful of **fresh cilantro** or **Thai basil leaves**
steamed jasmine rice, to serve

Remove the tough outer stems from the lemon grass, then cut into 1 inch pieces.

Put the coconut milk, stock, garlic, ginger, chile, lemon grass, sugar, and lime leaves in a large saucepan and bring to a boil. Add the sweet potatoes, cover, and simmer for 10 minutes.

Add the red bell pepper to the pan and cook for another 5 minutes.

Stir in the spinach and lime juice, replace the lid, and cook for 2–3 minutes, until the spinach has wilted, then stir in the cilantro or Thai basil. Serve immediately with steamed jasmine rice.

For Thai massaman vegetable curry, cut 12 oz scrubbed new potatoes into small pieces and cook in a saucepan of boiling water for 4 minutes, until just tender, then drain. Meanwhile, heat 1 tablespoon sunflower oil in a separate saucepan, add 3½ cups mixed chopped vegetables, such as carrots, green beans, and zucchini, and 3 tablespoons vegetarian Thai massaman curry paste and cook, stirring frequently, for 3–4 minutes. Pour in 1¾ cups coconut milk, stir in 2 kaffir lime leaves, and bring to a boil. Add the potatoes, then reduce the heat, cover, and simmer for 10 minutes, until the vegetables are tender. Serve garnished with a large handful of unsalted peanuts.

quick vegetable mole

Serves **4**
Preparation time **10 minutes**
Cooking time **30–35 minutes**

1 tablespoon **sunflower oil**
1 large **onion**, chopped
1 **garlic clove**, crushed
2 **sweet potatoes**, peeled and
   cut into small chunks
1 large **red bell pepper**,
   cored, seeded, and chopped
1 tablespoon **chili powder**
2 (14½ oz) cans **diced
   tomatoes**
⅔ cup **vegetable stock**
1 (15 oz) can **red kidney
   beans**, drained and rinsed
1 (15 oz) can **black beans**,
   drained and rinsed
½ oz **semisweet chocolate**,
   grated
2 tablespoons chopped **fresh
   cilantro**
salt and **black pepper**

To serve
cooked long-grain rice
sour cream

Heat the oil in a large saucepan, add the onion and garlic, and cook over medium heat for 2–3 minutes, until softened. Add the sweet potatoes and red bell pepper and cook for 2 minutes.

Stir in the chili powder, tomatoes, stock, and all the beans and bring to a boil. Reduce the heat, cover, and simmer gently for 20–25 minutes, until the vegetables are tender. Season to taste with salt and black pepper.

Add the chocolate and cilantro and cook for another 2–3 minutes. Serve with long-grain rice topped with spoonfuls of sour cream.

For Mexican bean soup, heat 1 tablespoon sunflower oil in a skillet, add 1 chopped onion, 1 chopped celery stick, 2 diced carrots, and 1 cored, seeded, and chopped red bell pepper and cook over medium heat for 5–6 minutes, until softened. Stir in 1 tablespoon chili powder, 1 (14½ oz) can diced tomatoes, 1 (15 oz) can each of red kidney beans and black beans, drained and rinsed, and 2½ cups hot vegetable stock. Simmer for 10 minutes. Stir in ½ oz grated semisweet chocolate and serve in bowls, garnished with chopped scallions, chopped fresh cilantro, and a spoonful of sour cream.

mango & coconut curry

Serves **4**

Preparation time **20 minutes**

Cooking time about **20 minutes**

4 cups grated **fresh coconut**

3–4 fresh **green chile**, coarsely chopped

1 tablespoon **cumin seeds**

2 cups **water**

3 firm ripe **mangoes**, peeled, pitted, and cubed

1 teaspoon **ground turmeric**

1 teaspoon **chili powder**

1¼ cups **fat-free plain yogurt**, lightly whisked

1 tablespoon **peanut oil**

2 teaspoons **black mustard seeds**

3–4 hot **dried red chiles**

10–12 **curry leaves**

Put the coconut, fresh chile, and cumin seeds in a food processor with half the measured water and blend to a fine paste.

Combine the mangoes with the turmeric, chili powder, and the remaining measured water in a heavy saucepan. Bring to a boil, add the coconut paste, and stir to mix well. Cover and simmer over medium heat for 10–12 minutes, stirring occasionally, until the mixture becomes fairly thick.

Add the yogurt and heat gently, stirring, until just warmed through. Do not let the mixture come to a boil or it will curdle. Remove from the heat and keep warm.

Heat the oil in a small skillet over medium-high heat. Add the mustard seeds and as soon as they begin to pop (after a few seconds), add the dried chiles and curry leaves. Stir-fry for a few seconds until the chiles darken. Stir into the mango curry and serve immediately.

chickpea & eggplant stew

Serves **4**
Preparation time **10 minutes**
Cooking time **45 minutes**

1 tablespoon **sunflower oil**
1 large **onion**, sliced
2 **garlic cloves**, crushed
1 teaspoon **ground cumin**
1 teaspoon **ground cinnamon**
1 teaspoon **ground turmeric**
1 teaspoon **ground paprika**
2 **eggplants**, chopped into
   1 ½ inch chunks
2 **carrots**, sliced
1 cup **soft dried pitted dates**
1 (14 ½ oz) can **diced
   tomatoes**
1 (15 oz) can **chickpeas**,
   drained and rinsed
2 ½ cups **vegetable stock**
4 slices of **preserved lemon**
2 tablespoons chopped **flat
   leaf parsley**
salt and **black pepper**
couscous, to serve

Heat the oil in a large saucepan, add the onion and garlic, and cook over medium heat for 4–5 minutes, until softened. Stir in all the spices and cook, stirring, for 1 minute.

Add the eggplants and cook for about 5 minutes, until starting to soften. Stir in all the remaining ingredients, except the parsley, and season to taste with salt and black pepper.

Bring to a boil, then reduce the heat, cover, and simmer for 30 minutes, stirring occasionally.

Stir in the parsley, then serve in deep warmed bowls with couscous.

For chickpea, apricot & almond stew, cook the onion and garlic as above, then stir in 2 teaspoons harissa paste and 1 teaspoon ground cinnamon and cook, stirring, for 1 minute. Add the eggplants and cook as above, then add the remaining ingredients, using 1 cup dried apricots in place of the dates. Cook as above, then stir in the parsley, sprinkle with ½ cup toasted blanched almonds, and serve with couscous.

spinach & tomato dhal

Serves **4**

Preparation time **10 minutes**

Cooking time **1 hour**

1¼ cups **dried red split
lentils**, rinsed and drained

½ teaspoon **ground turmeric**

2 **green chile**, seeded and
chopped

2 teaspoons peeled and
grated **fresh ginger root**

4 cups **water**

1 (14½ oz) can **diced
tomatoes**

1 (6 oz) package **baby
spinach leaves**

salt

Spiced oil

1 tablespoon **sunflower oil**

1 **shallot**, thinly sliced

12 **curry leaves**

1 teaspoon **black mustard
seeds**

1 teaspoon **cumin seeds**

1 **dried red chile**, broken into
small pieces

Place the lentils in a large saucepan with the turmeric,
chile, ginger, and measured water. Bring to a boil, then
reduce the heat and simmer, uncovered, for 40 minutes
or until the lentils have broken down and the mixture
has thickened.

Add the tomatoes and cook for another 10 minutes
or until thickened. Stir in the spinach and cook for
2–3 minutes, until wilted.

Prepare the spiced oil. Heat the oil in a small skillet,
add the shallot, and cook over medium-high heat,
stirring, for 2–3 minutes, until golden brown. Add all
the remaining ingredients and cook, stirring constantly,
for 1–2 minutes, until the seeds start to pop.

Add the spiced oil to the dhal, stir well, and season
to taste with salt. Serve with naan or steamed
long-grain rice, if desired.

For coconut & spinach dhal, follow the recipe above
to cook the lentils with the turmeric, chile, ginger,
and measured water for 40 minutes. Continue as
above, using 1 cup coconut milk and 4 chopped fresh
tomatoes in place of the canned diced tomatoes. Serve
the dhal with naan.

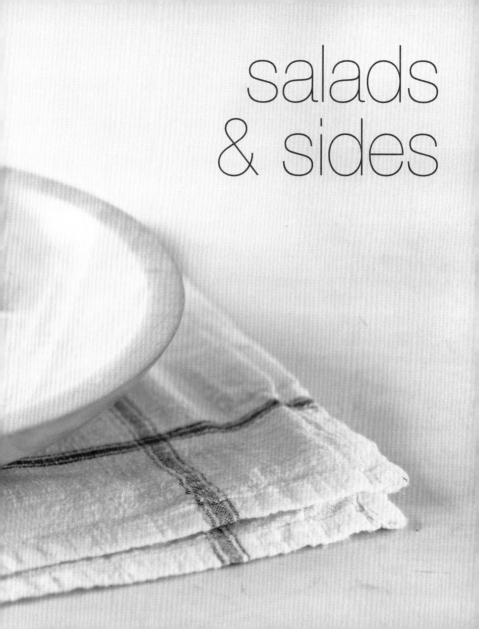

salads & sides

crisp parsnip cakes

Serves **4**
Preparation time **10 minutes**
Cooking time **20–25 minutes**

6 **parsnips**, peeled
  and chopped
4 tablespoons **butter**
1 **garlic clove**, crushed
1 tablespoon chopped **thyme**
2 tablespoons **sunflower oil**
salt and **black pepper**

Cook the parsnips in a large saucepan of lightly salted boiling water for 10 minutes, until tender.

Meanwhile, melt the butter in a small skillet, add the garlic and thyme, and cook gently, stirring, for 2 minutes.

Drain the parsnips, return to the pan, and mash thoroughly. Mash in the buttery garlic mixture and season well with salt and black pepper. Let stand until cool enough to handle.

Shape the parsnip mixture into 8 patties with lightly floured hands.

Heat 1 tablespoon of the oil in a large skillet, add 4 of the patties, and cook for 3–4 minutes on each side until golden brown. Transfer the patties to a baking sheet and keep warm in a low oven while you repeat with the remaining oil and patties. Serve warm.

For curried parsnip patties, cook the parsnips as above. Melt 4 tablespoons butter in a skillet, add 1 crushed garlic clove and 1 tablespoon medium curry powder, and cook, stirring, for 2 minutes. Drain the parsnips, return to the pan, and mash thoroughly. Beat in the spiced butter mixture with 2 tablespoons chopped fresh cilantro. Shape into patties and cook as above.

cannellini & green bean salad

Serves **4**
Preparation time **15 minutes**
Cooking time **12–15 minutes**

12 oz small **new potatoes**,
   scrubbed and halved
2 cups halved, trimmed **fine
   green beans**
1 (15 oz) can **cannellini
   beans**, drained and rinsed
¾ cup **pitted ripe black
   olives**, sliced
½ small **red onion**, thinly
   sliced
¼ cup **extra virgin olive oil**
grated zest and juice of
   1 large **lemon**
pinch of **sugar**
2 tablespoons chopped **mint**
2 tablespoons chopped
   parsley
salt and **black pepper**

Cook the potatoes in a large saucepan of boiling water
for 12–15 minutes, until tender, adding the green beans
for the last 3 minutes. Drain and refresh under cold
running water.

Put the cannellini beans, olives, and onion into a large
bowl and stir in the potatoes and green beans.

Whisk together the oil, lemon zest and juice, sugar, and
salt and black pepper in a small bowl, then stir in the
chopped herbs. Pour the dressing over the bean and
potato mixture and toss well before serving.

For white bean & tomato salad, put 2 (15 oz)
cans cannellini or lima beans, drained and rinsed,
in a bowl and stir in 16 halved vine cherry tomatoes
and 2 tablespoons chopped flat leaf parsley. Whisk
together ¼ cup extra virgin olive oil, the juice of
1 lemon, 1 teaspoon Dijon mustard, and 1 crushed
garlic clove in a small bowl. Season to taste with salt
and black pepper. Pour the dressing over the bean and
tomato mixture and gently toss together. Serve with
toasted ciabatta, if desired.

herb-roasted new potatoes

Serves **6**

Preparation time **10 minutes**

Cooking time **45–50 minutes**

2 tablespoons **olive oil**

2 lb **new potatoes**, scrubbed

4 **garlic cloves**, peeled but
   left whole

2 **rosemary sprigs**

2 **thyme sprigs**

1 **sage sprig**

sea salt and **black pepper**

Put the oil into a roasting pan and place in a preheated oven, at 400°F, for 5 minutes until hot.

Add the potatoes, garlic cloves, and herb sprigs, season well with sea salt and black pepper, and turn to coat in the oil.

Return to the oven and roast for 40–45 minutes, turning occasionally, until the potatoes are crisp and tender. Serve hot.

For crushed new potatoes with scallions & mustard, cook 2 lb scrubbed new potatoes in a large saucepan of lightly salted boiling water for 15 minutes or until tender. Drain well, return to the pan, and add 2 tablespoons olive oil and 1 tablespoon whole-grain mustard. Crush with a fork until the potatoes are broken up but not mashed, then stir in 4 chopped scallions. Season to taste with salt and black pepper and serve immediately.

roast tomato & mozzarella salad

Serves **4**
Preparation time **10 minutes**,
 plus cooling
Cooking time **20 minutes**

16 **baby plum** or **cherry
 tomatoes**, halved
1 tablespoon **olive oil**
5 oz **mini mozzarella balls**,
 drained
3 tablespoons **pine nuts**,
 toasted
sea salt and **black pepper**
ciabatta, to serve

Dressing
1 cup **arugula leaves**
12 **basil leaves**
¼ cup **extra virgin olive oil**
1 teaspoon **red wine vinegar**

Place the tomatoes, cut side up, in a small roasting pan. Drizzle the olive oil over them and season with a little sea salt and black pepper. Roast in a preheated oven, at 400°F, for 20 minutes, until wilted and softened. Remove from the oven and let cool.

Make the dressing. Place the arugula and basil leaves, 2 tablespoons of the extra virgin olive oil, and the vinegar in a small bowl. Blend with an immersion blender to a puree, or transfer to a mini food processor to blend. Stir in the remaining oil and season to taste with salt and black pepper.

Arrange the roasted tomatoes on a plate, then tear the mozzarella balls in half and arrange among the tomatoes. Drizzle with the dressing and sprinkle with the pine nuts. Serve immediately with ciabatta.

For basil dressing, to serve as an alternative dressing for the salad, use ¾ cup basil leaves in place of the arugula and basil and follow the recipe above to prepare the dressing. Serve the salad with a handful of arugula leaves.

ginger, coconut & lime leaf rice

Serves **4**
Preparation time **10 minutes**,
  plus standing
Cooking time **15 minutes**

1 ⅓ cups **jasmine rice**
2 teaspoons peeled and
  chopped **fresh ginger root**
1 ¼ cups **coconut milk**
6 **kaffir lime leaves**, bashed
1 **lemon grass stalk**, halved
  and bruised
1 teaspoon **salt**
1 cup **water**

Put the rice in a strainer and rinse in cold water until the
water runs clear. Drain and shake well.

Combine the rice with all the remaining ingredients in
a saucepan with a tight-fitting lid. Bring to a boil, cover
with the lid, and cook over low heat for 10 minutes.

Remove from the heat and let stand, covered and
without stirring, for 10 minutes. Fluff up with a fork
before serving.

For cardamom & lemon rice, rinse and drain
1 ⅓ cups basmati rice or other long-grain rice as
above. Heat 1 tablespoon sunflower oil in a large
saucepan with a tight-fitting lid, add 1 chopped onion,
and cook gently for 2–3 minutes, until softened. Stir
in 6 crushed cardamom pods and the rice and stir-fry
for 2–3 minutes, then pour in 2 cups boiling water.
Season with salt and stir well, then cover with the lid
and cook over low heat for 10 minutes. Remove from
the heat and stir in the juice of 2 lemons. Let stand,
covered and without stirring, for 10 minutes. Fluff up
with a fork before serving.

apple, blue cheese & nut salad

Serves **4**

Preparation time **15 minutes**, plus cooling

Cooking time **10–12 minutes**

1 tablespoon **unsalted butter**

2 tablespoons **sugar**

2 **sweet, crisp red apples**, cored and cut into thin wedges

¾ cup **walnut pieces**

½ small **red cabbage**, thinly sliced

2 **celery sticks**, chopped

1 cup crumbled **vegetarian blue cheese**, such as dolcelatte

walnut bread, to serve

Dressing

2 tablespoons **walnut oil**

2 tablespoons **olive oil**

2 tablespoons **balsamic vinegar**

salt and **black pepper**

Melt the butter in a skillet, add the sugar, and stir over low heat until the sugar has dissolved.

Add the apples to the pan and cook for 3–4 minutes on each side until they start to caramelize, then stir in the walnuts and cook for 1 minute. Remove from the heat and let cool.

Put the red cabbage and celery into a bowl, then add the cooled apple and walnut mixture.

Make the dressing. Put the oils and vinegar into a screw-top jar with salt and black pepper to taste, add the lid, and shake well.

Drizzle the dressing over the ingredients in the bowl and toss together. Serve immediately, sprinkled with the blue cheese, with the walnut bread.

For pear, spinach & Stilton salad, melt the butter and heat the sugar until dissolved as above. Add 2 cored and thinly sliced firm but ripe pears in place of the apples and cook until caramelized, then stir in the walnuts as above. Put 1 (6 oz) package baby spinach leaves into a bowl, instead of the red cabbage and celery, and add the pear and walnut mixture. Prepare the dressing as above, add to the bowl, and gently coat the salad ingredients in the dressing. Sprinkle with 1 cup crumbled Stilton and serve the salad immediately.

mashed sweet potato & garlic

Serves **4**
Preparation time **10 minutes**
Cooking time **20 minutes**

6 **sweet potatoes** (about
  2 lb), peeled and cut into
  1 inch pieces
4–6 **smoked garlic cloves**,
  peeled but left whole
2 tablespoons **salted butter**
2 tablespoons **milk**
2 tablespoons chopped **flat
  leaf parsley**
salt and **black pepper**

Put the sweet potatoes and smoked garlic cloves into a large saucepan, cover with cold water, and bring to a boil. Reduce the heat and simmer for 10–12 minutes, until tender, then drain well.

Return the sweet potatoes and garlic to the pan and mash until smooth.

Set the pan over low heat, then push the mashed ingredients to one side, add the butter to the bottom of the pan, and let melt. Pour the milk onto the butter and heat for 1–2 minutes, then beat into the mashed ingredients.

Stir in the parsley, season to taste with salt and black pepper, and serve.

For mashed sweet potato, cheese & mustard, cook the potatoes as above, omitting the smoked garlic, then beat in the butter and milk with 2 tablespoons whole-grain mustard and 1 cup shredded sharp cheddar cheese. Stir in 2 tablespoons chopped chives, season to taste with salt and black pepper, and serve.

thai rice salad

Serves **4**
Preparation time **20 minutes**

2 cups freshly cooked mixed
  long-grain and **wild rice**,
  cooled
2 **carrots**, thinly sliced
½ **cucumber**, halved, seeded,
  and thinly sliced
1 **red bell pepper**, cored,
  seeded, and thinly sliced
¾ cups **bean sprouts**
4 **scallions**, thinly sliced
¼ cup chopped **fresh cilantro**
⅓ cup **roasted unsalted
  peanuts**, coarsely chopped
lime wedges, to serve

Dressing
¼ cup **sweet chili sauce**
grated zest and juice of
  2 **limes**
2 teaspoons **light soy sauce**

Put the cooked rice, carrots, cucumber, red bell pepper, bean sprouts, scallions, and cilantro into a large bowl and mix together thoroughly.

Make the dressing. Whisk together all the dressing ingredients in a small bowl, then pour them over the salad and toss to coat.

Sprinkle the peanuts over the salad and serve immediately with lime wedges.

For Vietnamese rice noodle salad, prepare 6 oz dried rice noodles in a large heatproof bowl according to the package directions, then drain and refresh under cold running water. Let drain. Put the carrots, cucumber, red bell pepper, bean sprouts, scallions, and peanuts into a large bowl as above and add the drained noodles. Whisk together ¼ cup lime juice, 3 tablespoons sweet chili sauce, 2 tablespoons rice wine vinegar, and 1 tablespoon light soy sauce in a small bowl, pour the dressing over the noodle mixture, and toss to coat. Stir in ¼ cup each of chopped mint and fresh cilantro. Serve in bowls, garnished with mint leaves.

mustard grilled potatoes

Serves **2**

Preparation time **10 minutes**,
plus standing

Cooking time **25 minutes**

1 lb **russet potatoes**,
scrubbed and cut into
½ inch thick slices

2 tablespoons **olive oil**

½ teaspoon **sea salt**

2 teaspoons **whole-grain
mustard**

1 tablespoon chopped
tarragon

sea salt and **black pepper**

Cook the potatoes in a saucepan of lightly salted boiling water for 10 minutes. Drain well and let dry for a few minutes.

Put 1 tablespoon of the oil in a large bowl with the teaspoon sea salt and a generous grinding of black pepper, add the potatoes, and turn gently to coat in the oil.

Heat a large, ridged grill pan over medium heat, and when hot, add the potatoes in a single layer. Cook for 3 minutes on each side, until golden. Remove and keep warm while you cook any remaining potatoes.

Whisk together the remaining oil, mustard, and tarragon in a small bowl. Put the potatoes into a shallow bowl and pour the dressing over them. Serve immediately.

For paprika grilled potatoes, cook the potatoes in boiling water, then drain well and let dry as above. Mix 2 tablespoons olive oil with 1–2 teaspoons smoked paprika and a little salt and black pepper in a large bowl. Add the potatoes and stir gently to coat in the paprika oil. Cook in a large, ridged grill pan as above and serve sprinkled with chopped flat leaf parsley.

breads & baking

quick mediterranean focaccia

Serves **8**
Preparation time **15 minutes**
Cooking time **15 minutes**

olive oil, for brushing
3⅔ cups **all-purpose flour**
1 teaspoon **baking soda**
1 teaspoon **salt**
1 tablespoon chopped
   rosemary, plus 10 small
   sprigs
1 (3½ oz) package **sun-dried
   tomatoes**, chopped
1¾ cups **buttermilk**
10 pitted **ripe black olives**
1 teaspoon **sea salt**

Brush a 9 inch x 12½ inch jellyroll pan with oil.

Sift the flour, baking soda, and salt into a large bowl. Stir in the chopped rosemary and sun-dried tomatoes. Make a well in the center, add the buttermilk to the well, and gradually stir into the flour. Bring the mixture together with your hands to form a soft, slightly sticky dough.

Transfer the dough to a lightly floured surface and lightly knead for 1 minute, then quickly roll into a rectangular shape to fit the prepared pan. Press the dough gently into the pan, then brush with oil. Using your finger, make small dimples in the top of the bread. Sprinkle with the black olives, rosemary sprigs, and sea salt.

Bake in a preheated oven, at 425°F, for 15 minutes, until brown and crisp. Brush with a little more olive oil and serve warm.

For cheese & onion focaccia, prepare the bread as above, omitting the sun-dried tomatoes and rosemary. Spread ½ finely sliced red onion and ¼ cup freshly grated vegetarian cheese over the top and bake as above.

spinach, feta & egg tarts

Makes **4**
Preparation time **15 minutes**
Cooking time **16–18 minutes**

1 (10 oz) package **frozen spinach**, defrosted
1 cup diced **feta cheese**
2 tablespoons **mascarpone cheese**
pinch of freshly grated **nutmeg**
4 sheets of **phyllo pastry**, defrosted if frozen
4 tablespoons **butter**, melted
4 **eggs**
salt and **black pepper**

Drain the spinach and squeeze out all the excess water, then chop finely if not already chopped. Place in a bowl and mix in the feta, mascarpone, nutmeg, and salt and black pepper to taste.

Lay the sheets of phyllo pastry on top of one another in a pile, brushing each with a little melted butter. Cut out four 6 inch circles, using a saucer as a template.

Divide the spinach mixture among the pastry circles, spreading the filling out but leaving a 1 inch border. Gather the edges up and over the filling to form a rim. Make a shallow well in the spinach mixture.

Transfer the tarts to a baking sheet and bake in a preheated oven, at 400°F, for 8 minutes. Remove from the oven and carefully crack an egg into each hollow. Bake for another 8–10 minutes, until the eggs are set.

For spinach & goat cheese packages, prepare the spinach as above, then mix with 4 oz soft goat cheese, 2 tablespoons mascarpone cheese, a pinch of ground cumin, and salt and black pepper to taste. Cut out the phyllo pastry circles as above and divide the spinach mixture among them, but place it on one half of each circle. Carefully fold the pastry over the filling and turn the pastry edges over to seal. Bake in the oven as above and serve with lemon wedges for squeezing over and Greek yogurt.

sweet potato & onion seed rolls

Makes **8**

Preparation time **30 minutes**,
  plus standing and rising

Cooking time **30–35 minutes**

2 **sweet potatoes**, peeled
  and chopped
1 tablespoon **olive oil**
1 teaspoon **active dry yeast**
2¼ cups **white bread flour**
½ teaspoon **salt**
½ teaspoon **ground black
  pepper**
1 teaspoon **black onion
  seeds**

Cook the sweet potatoes in a saucepan of boiling water for about 15 minutes, until tender. Drain, reserving ⅓ cup of the cooking water. Return the potatoes to the pan and set over low heat to dry off the excess water, then mash with the oil.

Put the reserved cooking water into a small bowl and, while still warm (but not hot), add the yeast and stir to dissolve. Let stand in a warm place for about 10 minutes, until bubbles appear on the surface.

Stir the yeast mixture into the potatoes, then gradually stir in the remaining ingredients to form a dough. Transfer the dough to a lightly floured surface and knead for 5 minutes, until smooth, then place in a lightly oiled bowl, cover with oiled plastic wrap, and let rise in a warm place for 45 minutes–1 hour.

Punch down the dough and then divide into 8 pieces. Shape into balls, then flatten slightly. Transfer to a lightly oiled baking sheet and cover loosely with oiled plastic wrap. Let rise for 30 minutes.

Bake in a preheated oven at 425°F, for 15–20 minutes, until risen and golden brown and hollow when tapped on the bottom. Transfer to a wire rack and let cool for 5 minutes before serving.

For sweet potato & rosemary loaf, prepare the dough as above, using 2 tablespoons chopped rosemary in place of the onion seeds. Let rise as above for 45 minutes–1 hour, then punch down the dough and shape into a large round loaf. Score the top with a serrated knife, place on a lightly oiled baking sheet, and bake as above for about 35 minutes.

shallot tarte tatin

Serves **4**
Preparation time **20 minutes**,
  plus cooling
Cooking time **40–45 minutes**

1 lb **shallots**, peeled but
  left whole
4 tablespoons **butter**
2 tablespoons packed **light
  brown sugar**
3 tablespoons **cider vinegar**
a few **thyme sprigs**
1 sheet **prepared puff pastry**,
  defrosted if frozen
salt and **black pepper**
arugula leaves, to serve

Cut any large shallots in half. Melt the butter in a flameproof 8 inch skillet, add the shallots, and cook over medium heat for 5 minutes, until just beginning to brown. Add the sugar and cook for another 5 minutes or until the shallots are caramelized, turning occasionally so that they cook evenly.

Stir in the vinegar, the leaves from the thyme sprigs, and salt and black pepper to taste and cook for 2 minutes.

Let the shallots cool for 20 minutes in the pan if it has a heatproof handle; if not, transfer to a heavy 8 inch round greased cake pan.

Roll out the pastry on a lightly floured surface and trim to an 8 inch circle. Arrange on top of the onions and tuck down the sides of the skillet or cake pan.

Bake in a preheated oven, at 400°F, for 25–30 minutes, until the pastry is well risen and golden. Let stand for 5 minutes, then loosen the edges with a knife. Cover with a serving plate or cutting board, invert the pan or cake pan onto the plate, and then remove. Serve warm, cut into wedges, with a green leaf salad.

For shallot, apple & walnut tarte Tatin, follow the recipe above, reducing the shallots to 12 oz and adding 1 crisp, sweet apple, cored, peeled, and cut into 8 slices. Continue as above, adding 2 tablespoons walnut pieces with the sugar.

spiced flatbreads

Makes **4**
Preparation time **15 minutes**
Cooking time **6 minutes**

2 teaspoons **cumin seeds**
1 teaspoon **coriander seeds**
3⅓ cups **white bread flour**
2¼ teaspoons **fast active yeast**
1 teaspoon **sugar**
1 teaspoon **sea salt**
1 tablespoon **olive oil**
1 cup plus 2 tablespoons **warm water**

Toast the cumin and coriander seeds in a dry skillet over medium heat until aromatic, then crush with a mortar and pestle.

Mix together the flour, yeast, sugar, salt, and toasted spices in a large bowl. Make a well in the center, add the oil to the well, and gradually stir into the flour with enough of the measured water to form a moist, pliable dough.

Transfer the dough to a lightly floured surface and knead for 5 minutes, until smooth and elastic. Divide into 4 balls and roll out thinly on a lightly floured surface into long oval or round shapes. Prick all over with a fork and arrange on nonstick baking sheets.

Bake in a preheated oven, at 425°F, for 3 minutes. Turn over and bake for another 3 minutes, until golden brown. Serve immediately or wrap in a dish towel or aluminum foil to keep warm before serving.

For Eastern spiced garlic flatbreads, prepare the dough as above, omitting the cumin and coriander seeds and stirring in 2 teaspoons baharat or zahtar spice mix and 2 crushed garlic cloves. Shape and bake as above.

margherita biscuit-crust pizza

Serves **4**
Preparation time **10 minutes**,
  plus cooling
Cooking time **20 minutes**

Pizza sauce
1 cup **tomato puree** or
  tomato sauce
2 tablespoons **tomato paste**
½ teaspoon **sugar**
1 teaspoon **dried mixed
  herbs**

Pizza crust
1¾ cups **all-purpose flour**
1¾ teaspoons **baking powder**
1 teaspoon **salt**
4 tablespoons **butter**, diced
⅔ cup **milk**

Topping
¼ cup shredded **cheddar
  cheese**
8 oz **mozzarella cheese**,
  drained and sliced
2 **tomatoes**, sliced
2 tablespoons fresh **pesto
  sauce** (see page 134
  for homemade)
basil leaves, to garnish

Put all the ingredients for the sauce into a small saucepan and simmer over low heat, stirring occasionally, for 5 minutes. Let cool.

Meanwhile, make the crust. Put the flour, baking powder, and salt into a large bowl, then rub in the butter with your fingertips. Slowly pour in the milk and mix to form a soft dough.

Roll out the dough thinly on a large, lightly oiled baking sheet into a 12 inch circle. Spread the pizza sauce over the pizza crust and sprinkle with the cheddar. Arrange the mozzarella and tomatoes over the top and drizzle with the pesto.

Bake in a preheated oven, at 400°F, for 15 minutes, until the crust is crisp and the cheese has melted. Serve hot with basil leaves sprinkled over the top.

For feta, spinach & black olive pizza, follow the recipe above to prepare the pizza sauce and pizza crust. Put 5 cups spinach leaves in a colander and pour over a saucepan of boiling water to wilt the leaves, then refresh under cold running water, drain, and squeeze out the excess water. Arrange over the pizza crust and top with 1 cup chopped feta cheese and ½ cup pitted ripe black olives. Bake as above.

blue cheese & thyme straws

Makes **40**
Preparation time **15 minutes**
Cooking time **15 minutes**

¾ cup **all-purpose flour**
2 teaspoons finely chopped
   thyme, plus extra
   for scattering
1 stick **unsalted butter**, chilled
   and diced
4 oz **firm blue cheese**, rind
   removed and grated
1 **egg yolk**
sea salt

Put the flour and thyme in a bowl or food processor. Add the butter and rub in with the fingertips or pulse until the mixture resembles bread crumbs. Stir in the blue cheese and egg yolk and mix or process briefly to a dough.

Transfer the dough to a lightly floured surface and lightly knead until smooth, then roll out into a rectangle ¼ inch thick. Cut into strips about ¼ inch wide and 3½ inches long.

Place slightly apart on a greased baking sheet. Sprinkle with sea salt and bake in a preheated oven, at 400°F, for about 15 minutes, until golden.

Let cool slightly on the baking sheet, then transfer to a wire rack to cool completely. Serve sprinkled with extra thyme.

For olive twists, roll out a sheet of prepared puff pastry, defrosted if frozen, on a lightly floured surface into a 10 inch x 6 inch rectangle and cut in half. Beat 1 egg yolk with 1 tablespoon water, then brush thinly over one half. Spread thinly with 3 tablespoons black or green olive tapenade. Place the second piece on top and roll again to make a 10 inch square. Trim the edges and brush the surface with more of the egg yolk mixture. Cut the pastry in half, then cut each half across into ¾ inch strips. Twist each strip several times, then place on a lightly greased baking sheet. Sprinkle with sea salt and bake as above.

caper & cheese corn muffins

Makes **10**
Preparation time **10 minutes**
Cooking time **20–25 minutes**

1 ⅓ cups **all-purpose flour**
2 teaspoons **baking powder**
½ cup **cornmeal**
2 tablespoons chopped **flat leaf parsley**
1 cup shredded **sharp cheddar cheese**
2 tablespoons **capers,** drained and rinsed
1 teaspoon **salt**
1 teaspoon **ground black pepper**
1 extra-large **egg**
6 tablespoons **butter,** melted
1 cup **milk**

Line a 12-section muffin pan with 10 paper liners.

Sift together the flour and baking powder into a large bowl. Add the cornmeal, parsley, three-quarters of the cheese, the capers, salt, and black pepper and mix well.

Beat together the egg, melted butter, and milk in a separate bowl. Pour the liquid ingredients over the dry ingredients and stir until only just combined; the batter should be lumpy.

Spoon the batter into the muffin liners so that they are about three-quarters full, then sprinkle the tops with the remaining cheese. Bake in a preheated oven, at 375°F, for 20–25 minutes, until risen and firm.

Let cool in the pan for 5 minutes, then transfer to a wire rack to continue cooling. Serve warm.

For olive, goat cheese & basil muffins, follow the above recipe to make the muffin batter, omitting the parsley and capers, and using 1 cup grated hard goat cheese in place of the cheddar. Stir in 1 cup chopped pitted ripe black or green olives and 2 tablespoons chopped basil with the wet ingredients. Bake as above.

squash, sage & roquefort pie

Serves **6**
Preparation time **20 minutes**
Cooking time **35–40 minutes**

1 **butternut squash**, peeled,
   seeded, and cut into cubes
2 small **red onions**, quartered
1 tablespoon **olive oil**
4 tablespoons **butter**, melted
10 sheets of **phyllo pastry**,
   defrosted if frozen
small bunch of **sage**
1 cup **ricotta cheese**
4 oz **Roquefort cheese**
salt and **black pepper**
arugula leaves, to serve

Spread the butternut squash and onions out in a roasting pan. Drizzle with the oil and season with black pepper. Roast in a preheated oven, at 375°F, for 15–20 minutes, until just tender.

Meanwhile, brush an 11 inch round loose-bottom tart pan with some of the melted butter. Lay a few sheets of phyllo pastry across it, slightly overlapping. Brush the overhanging phyllo with more butter. Continue layering the remaining phyllo, buttering as you work and slightly overlapping the sides of the pan.

Chop the sage coarsely, reserving 6 leaves. Mix together the ricotta and chopped sage in a bowl and season well with salt and black pepper, then spoon into the phyllo pastry shell. Spoon over the roasted squash and onions, then crumble over the Roquefort and sprinkle with the reserved sage leaves.

Bake the pie in the oven for 20 minutes, until golden. Serve warm with arugula leaves.

For Greek spinach, feta & pine nut pie, prepare the phyllo pastry shell as above. Mix together ¾ cup ricotta cheese and 1 cup feta cheese, 8 cups baby spinach leaves, the juice of 1 lemon, 3 tablespoons pine nuts, 1 tablespoon raisins, and 1 crushed garlic clove in a large bowl, and season well with salt and black pepper. Spoon into the phyllo pastry shell and bake as above.

banana & pecan loaf

Serves **8–10**
Preparation time **10 minutes**
Cooking time **50–60 minutes**

1 stick **butter**, softened
1 cup firmly packed **light
 brown sugar**
2 **eggs**
4 **ripe bananas**, mashed
½ cup **buttermilk**
1 teaspoon **vanilla extract**
1 ¾ cups **all-purpose flour**
1 teaspoon **baking soda**
1 teaspoon **baking powder**
½ teaspoon **salt**
1 cup coarsely chopped
 pecans, plus 8 halves
 to decorate

Grease a 9 x 5 x 3 inch loaf pan. Beat the butter and sugar together in a large bowl with a handheld electric mixer until pale and fluffy.

Beat in the eggs, mashed bananas, buttermilk, and vanilla extract until well combined.

Sift the flour, baking soda, baking powder, and salt over the wet ingredients and gently fold in with a large metal spoon, then stir in the chopped pecans.

Spoon the batter into the prepared pan and arrange the pecan halves down the center.

Bake in a preheated oven, at 350°F, for 50–60 minutes or until risen and golden brown and a toothpick inserted into the center comes out clean. Cover the top of the loaf with aluminum foil if it starts becoming too brown before the end of the baking time.

Let the loaf cool in the pan for a few minutes, then turn out onto a wire rack to cool completely before serving.

For banana, golden raisin & walnut bread, follow the recipe above, using 1 cup chopped walnuts in place of the pecans and stirring in 1 cup golden raisins with the nuts. Arrange 8 walnut halves down the center of the loaf and bake as above.

walnut & white chocolate cookies

Makes about **25**
Preparation time **15 minutes**
Cooking time **12–15 minutes**

1 **egg**
¾ cup firmly packed **light brown sugar**
2 tablespoons **granulated sugar**
1 teaspoon **vanilla extract**
½ cup **vegetable oil**
⅔ cup **all-purpose flour**
¼ teaspoon **baking powder**
¼ teaspoon **ground cinnamon**
⅓ cup **shredded dry coconut**
1½ cups **walnut pieces, toasted and chopped**
¾ cup **white chocolate chips**

Brush 2 baking sheets lightly with oil and line with nonstick parchment paper.

Beat together the egg and sugars in a bowl until pale and creamy. Stir in the vanilla extract and oil. Sift in the flour, baking powder, and cinnamon, then add the coconut, walnuts, and chocolate chips and mix well with a wooden spoon.

Shape rounded tablespoonfuls of the dough into balls and place on the prepared baking sheets, pressing the mixture together with your fingertips if it is crumbly. Bake in a preheated oven, at 350°F, for 12–15 minutes or until golden.

Let cool for a few minutes on the sheets, then transfer to a wire rack to cool completely.

For hazelnut & chocolate chip cookies, follow the recipe above to make the cookie dough, using ½ teaspoon ground ginger in place of the cinnamon, toasted and chopped hazelnuts instead of the walnuts, and semisweet chocolate chips in place of the white. Shape and bake as above.

tropical fruitcake

Serves **12**
Preparation time **15 minutes**,
plus cooling
Cooking time **1 hour–
1 hour 10 minutes**

⅔ cup **raisins**
1½ cups chopped **mixed
dried tropical fruit**, such
as pineapple, mango,
papaya, and apricots
1 teaspoon **ground allspice**
1 teaspoon **ground ginger**
1 stick **unsalted butter**, cut
into cubes
½ cup firmly packed **light
brown sugar**
⅔ cup **cold water**
1¾ cups **all-purpose flour**
1¾ teaspoons **baking powder**
1 **egg**, lightly beaten

Grease and line the bottom of a 9 x 5 x 3 inch loaf pan
with nonstick parchment paper (or use a loaf pan liner).

Put the raisins, dried tropical fruit, allspice, ginger,
butter, sugar, and measured water into a saucepan.
Warm over low heat until the butter has melted, stirring
occasionally with a wooden spoon, then bring to a boil.

Boil the fruit mixture for 5 minutes, then remove from
the heat and let cool in the pan.

Stir the flour, baking powder, and beaten egg into the
cooled fruit mixture until well combined, then spoon into
the prepared pan.

Bake in the center of a preheated oven, at 300°F, for
50–60 minutes or until a toothpick inserted into the
center comes out clean.

Let the cake cool in the pan, then cut into slices
to serve.

For traditional fruitcake, follow the recipe above to
make the cake batter, using a mixture of dried currants,
chopped dried pitted dates, golden raisins, and candied
cherries in place of the dried tropical fruit and omitting
the ground ginger. Bake as above.

apricot & cheese soda bread

Serves **8**
Preparation time **10 minutes**,
  plus cooling
Cooking time **35–40 minutes**

2 teaspoons **sunflower oil**
6 **scallions**, thinly sliced
2 cups **all-purpose flour**
2 cups **whole-wheat flour**
2 teaspoons **baking soda**
1 teaspoon **salt**
¾ cup shredded **mild
  cheddar cheese**
¼ cup chopped **dried
  apricots**
1¾ cups **buttermilk**, plus
  2 tablespoons for brushing

Heat the oil in a small skillet, add the scallions, and cook gently for 2 minutes, until softened. Let cool slightly.

Sift the flours, baking soda, and salt into a large bowl. Stir in the cheese, apricots, and scallions. Make a well in the center, add the buttermilk to the well, and gradually stir into the flour. Bring the mixture together with your hands to form a soft, slightly sticky dough.

Transfer the dough to a lightly floured surface and lightly knead for 1 minute, then shape into a ball.

Place on a lightly floured nonstick baking sheet and flatten slightly. Make a deep cross in the top with a serrated knife. Brush the top with the remaining buttermilk.

Bake in a preheated oven, at 400°F, for 30–35 minutes, until the loaf sounds hollow when tapped on the bottom. Let cool on a wire rack. It is best served warm.

For apple & cheese soda bread, follow the recipe above to make the dough, adding 2 peeled, cored, and chopped crisp, sweet apples and using 1 cup shredded sharp cheddar cheese in place of the mild cheddar cheese and apricots. Bake as above.

giant choc chip-orange cookies

Makes **12**
Preparation time **20 minutes**,
  plus chilling
Cooking time **10–12 minutes**

½ cup **light brown sugar**
⅔ cup **granulated sugar**
1¼ sticks **butter**, softened
2 teaspoons finely grated
  orange zest
1 extra-large **egg**, lightly
  beaten
1 teaspoon **vanilla extract**
2 cups **all-purpose flour**
1 teaspoon **baking powder**
5 oz good-quality **semisweet
  chocolate with orange**,
  coarsely chopped into
  chunks

Beat together the sugars, butter, and orange zest in a large bowl with a handheld electric mixer until smooth and pale. Add the beaten egg and vanilla extract and beat until combined.

Sift in the flour and baking powder and mix with a wooden spoon until all the ingredients are combined. Stir in the chocolate chunks and bring the mixture together with your hands to form a dough.

Transfer the cookie dough to a large sheet of plastic wrap, roll the dough into a wide 3 inch log shape, and wrap in the plastic wrap, twisting the ends to seal. Chill in the refrigerator for 30 minutes.

Slice the dough into about twelve ¾ inch thick disks and place, spaced apart, on 2 large nonstick baking sheets. Bake in a preheated oven, at 350°F, for 10–12 minutes or until golden brown around the edge and slightly paler in the center.

Let cool on the baking sheets for 2 minutes, then transfer to a wire rack to cool completely.

For white chocolate & macadamia nut cookies,
prepare the cookie dough as above, omitting the orange zest and using 4 oz coarsely chopped good-quality white chocolate in place of the semisweet chocolate and adding ⅓ cup chopped macadamia nuts. Shape and bake as above.

lime & coconut drizzle cake

Serves **8**
Preparation time **20 minutes**
Cooking time **35–40 minutes**

1¾ sticks **unsalted butter,**
  softened, plus extra
  for greasing
1 cup **granulated sugar**
finely grated zest and juice
  of 2 **limes**
3 **eggs**, lightly beaten
1⅔ cups **all-purpose flour,**
  sifted
1½ teaspoons **baking powder**
¾ cup **shredded dried**
  coconut

Topping
¼ cup **granulated sugar**
2 tablespoons **shredded**
  dried coconut
finely pared long strands
  of **lime zest**

Grease an 8 inch round springform cake pan and line the bottom with nonstick parchment paper.

Beat together the butter, sugar, and grated lime zest in a large bowl with a handheld electric mixer until pale and fluffy. Beat in the eggs a little at a time, adding 1 tablespoon of the flour if the mixture starts to curdle, then fold in the flour, baking powder, and coconut with a large metal spoon.

Spoon into the prepared pan and bake in the center of a preheated oven, at 350 °F, for 35–40 minutes, until risen and golden and shrinking away from the pan.

Let cool in the pan. While still warm, mix the sugar for the topping with the lime juice and spoon it over the cake. Sprinkle with the coconut and lime zest strands. Let cool completely.

For lime & coconut cupcakes, line a 12-section cupcake pan with paper liners. Beat together 1 stick softened butter, ⅔ cup granulated sugar, and the finely grated zest of 2 limes in a large bowl with a handheld electric mixer until pale and fluffy. Beat in 2 eggs and the juice of the limes. Fold in 1¼ cups all-purpose flour, 2 teaspoons baking powder, and ¾ cup shredded dried coconut. Divide among the paper liners. Bake in a preheated oven, at 350°F, for 15–20 minutes, until risen and golden. Let cool on a wire rack. Mix the grated zest and juice of 1 lime with 1⅓ cups confectioners' sugar and a few drops of green food coloring. Spoon the topping over the cakes and sprinkle with shredded dried coconut.

desserts

plum & frangipane tart

Serves **8**
Preparation time **25 minutes**
Cooking time **45–50 minutes**

1 sheet **prepared rolled
  dough pie cruist**, defrosted
  if frozen
⅓ cup **plum preserves**
1 ¼ sticks **unsalted butter**,
  softened
¾ cup **granulated sugar**
3 **eggs**, lightly beaten
2 cups **ground almonds
  (almond meal)**
½ teaspoon **almond extract**
¾ cup **all-purpose flour**
6 ripe **plums**, halved and
  pitted
¼ cup **slivered almonds**

Roll out the dough on a lightly floured surface and use to line a 9 inch) loose-bottom tart pan. Spread half the plum preserves over the bottom of the dough.

Beat together the butter and sugar in a large bowl with a handheld electric mixer until pale and fluffy. Gradually beat in the eggs, then stir in the ground almonds, almond extract, and flour. Spoon the almond mixture over the preserves in the pastry shell.

Arrange the plums, skin side up, in circles over the almond mixture, starting from the outside, until it is covered. Sprinkle with the slivered almonds.

Place on a preheated baking sheet and bake in a preheated oven, at 400°F, for 40–45 minutes, until risen and set.

Warm the remaining preserves in a small saucepan, then brush over the top of the tart while the tart is still warm. Serve the tart warm in slices with a spoonful of heavy cream.

For apricot & almond tart, follow the recipe above to make the tart, using apricot preserves in place of the plum preserves and 8–10 halved and pitted ripe apricots. Bake as above, then brush the top of the tart with the remaining warmed apricot preserves and serve in slices.

quick tiramisu

Serves **4–6**

Preparation time **15 minutes**, plus chilling

⅓ cup strong **espresso coffee**

⅓ cup firmly packed **dark brown sugar**

¼ cup **coffee liqueur** or 3 tablespoons **brandy**

6 **ladyfinger cookies**, broken into large pieces

1⅓ cups **prepared custard** or **prepared instant vanilla pudding and pie filling mix**

1 cup **mascarpone cheese**

1 teaspoon **vanilla extract**

3 oz **semisweet chocolate**, finely chopped

unsweetened ocoa powder, sifted, for dusting

Mix the coffee with 2 tablespoons of the sugar and the liqueur or brandy in a bowl. Toss the ladyfingers in the mixture and turn into a serving dish, spooning any excess liquid over the cookies.

Beat together the custard, mascarpone, and vanilla extract in a large bowl and spoon one-third of the mixture over the ladyfingers. Sprinkle with the remaining sugar, then spoon half the remaining custard over the top. Sprinkle with half the chopped chocolate, then spread with the remaining custard and sprinkle with the remaining chopped chocolate.

Chill for about 1 hour, until set. Dust with sifted cocoa powder and serve.

For raspberry tiramisu, put 1 cup raspberries in a saucepan with 1 tablespoon granulated sugar and 2 tablespoons water. Bring to a boil, then remove from the heat and beat with a wooden spoon to crush. Spoon into a strainer set over a bowl and press through the strainer to make a simple coulis. Prepare the other ingredients as above, omitting the coffee liqueur, and use the coulis to top the ladyfinger cookies before layering with the mascarpone and custard mixture. Add a layer of raspberries on top of the mascarpone. Dust with sifted unsweetened cocoa powder to serve.

pear & choc self-saucing cake

Serves **6**

Preparation time **15 minutes**

Cooking time **40–45 minutes**

4 ripe **pears**, peeled, cored, and sliced

1 cup **all-purpose flour**

¼ cup **unsweetened cocoa powder**

2 teaspoons **baking powder**

¾ cup **granulated sugar**

1 cup **milk**

6 tablespoons **butter**, melted

1 **egg**, lightly beaten

cream or **vanilla ice cream**, to serve

Chocolate sauce

1 cup **water**

1 cup firmly packed **light brown sugar**

1 tablespoon **unsweetened cocoa powder**, sifted

1 teaspoon **vanilla extract**

Arrange the pear slices in the bottom of a greased 1½ quart ovenproof dish.

Sift together the flour, cocoa powder, and baking powder into a large bowl and add the granulated sugar, milk, melted butter, and egg. Beat with a handheld electric mixer until smooth and creamy, then pour the mixture over the pears.

Combine all the sauce ingredients in a saucepan and heat over low heat, stirring, until the sugar has dissolved. Bring to a boil, then pour over the batter.

Bake in a preheated oven, at 350°F, for 35–40 minutes, until the cake is risen. Let stand for 3–4 minutes before serving. Serve with cream or vanilla ice cream.

For pear & caramel self-saucing cake, prepare the sponge batter as above, omitting the cocoa powder and reducing the granulated sugar to ⅔ cup. Pour the batter over the pears. For the caramel sauce, put ¾ cup firmly packed light brown sugar into a saucepan with ¼ cup light corn syrup and 1 cup water and heat over low heat, stirring, until the sugar has dissolved. Bring to a boil, then pour over the cake. Bake as above until risen and golden. Let stand for 5 minutes before serving.

pistachio chocolate brownies

Serves **6**
Preparation time **20 minutes**,
   plus cooling
Cooking time **30 minutes**

7 oz **semisweet chocolate**,
   broken into pieces
1¾ sticks **butter**, diced
1 cup firmly packed **light
   brown sugar**
3 **eggs**
⅓ cup **all-purpose flour**
1 teaspoon **baking powder**
⅓ cup coarsely chopped
   pistachio nuts
vanilla ice cream, to serve

Sauce
4 oz **semisweet chocolate**,
   broken into pieces
⅔ cup **low-fat milk**
2 tablespoons packed **light
   brown sugar**

Line an 8 inch square cake pan with nonstick parchment paper.

Melt together the chocolate and butter in a heatproof bowl set over a saucepan of gently simmering water, stirring occasionally, making sure that the water doesn't touch the bottom of the bowl.

Beat together the sugar and eggs in a large bowl with a handheld electric mixer until pale, thick, and the beaters leave a trail when lifted out of the mixture. Fold in the melted chocolate mixture, then the flour and baking powder.

Pour the batter into the prepared pan and sprinkle with the pistachios. Bake in a preheated oven, at 350°F, for about 25 minutes, until the top is crusty but the center is still slightly soft. Let cool and harden in the pan.

Make the sauce. Heat all the sauce ingredients together gently in a saucepan, stirring until smooth.

Lift the brownies out of the pan, using the paper. Cut into small squares, lift off the paper, and transfer to serving plates. Add scoops of vanilla ice cream and serve with the warm chocolate sauce.

For white chocolate & cranberry blondies, melt 7 oz white chocolate, broken into pieces, with 1 stick butter, diced, as above. Beat ¾ cup granulated sugar with 3 eggs as above, then fold in the melted chocolate mixture. Fold in 1¼ cups all-purpose flour, 1¼ teaspoons baking powder, and ⅓ cup dried cranberries. Bake as above.

chocolate & chili mousse cake

Serves **8–10**

Preparation time **20 minutes**,
plus cooling and chilling

Cooking time **35 minutes**

10 oz good-quality **semisweet
chocolate with chili**, broken
into pieces

1 ¼ sticks **unsalted butter**,
diced

6 **eggs**, separated

⅔ cup **granulated sugar**

Chili syrup

1 **red chile**, thinly sliced

grated zest and juice of **1 lime**

½ cup **granulated sugar**

⅔ cup **water**

Line the bottom of an 8 inch springform cake pan
with nonstick parchment paper. Melt the chocolate and
butter in a heatproof bowl set over a saucepan of gently
simmering water, stirring occasionally, making sure the
water doesn't touch the bottom of the bowl. Meanwhile,
beat the egg yolks with the sugar in a bowl with a
handheld electric mixer until pale and thick. Stir in the
melted chocolate mix.

Beat the egg whites in a separate large, grease-
free bowl until they form soft peaks. Fold a couple of
tablespoons of the egg white into the chocolate mixture
to loosen, then fold in the remaining egg white with a
metal spoon. Pour the batter into the prepared pan and
bake in a preheated oven, at 350°F, for 20 minutes.
Remove from the oven, cover with aluminum foil (to
prevent a crust from forming), and let cool. Chill in the
refrigerator for at least 4 hours or overnight.

Make the syrup. Combine all the syrup ingredients in
a small saucepan and heat over low heat, stirring, until
the sugar has dissolved. Bring to a boil, then simmer
for 10 minutes, until syrupy. Let cool. Remove the cake
from the refrigerator 30 minutes before serving in
slices, with the syrup poured over the top.

For chocolate, whiskey & ginger mousse cake,
prepare the cake batter as above, using 10 oz
semisweet chocolate with ginger, broken into pieces,
in place of the semisweet chocolate with chili and
adding 2 tablespoons whiskey. Bake, cool, and chill as
above. Beat 1 ¼ cups heavy cream with 1 tablespoon
whiskey and spoon the whipped cream over the cake.
Dust with unsweetened cocoa powder and serve.

melon, ginger & lime sorbet

Serves **4**

Preparation time **15 minutes**,
plus freezing

1 large ripe **honeydew melon**
or **canteloupe**, chilled

¾ cup **granulated sugar**

1 tablespoon peeled and finely
grated **fresh ginger root**

juice of 2 **limes**

Cut the melon in half and remove and discard the seeds, then coarsely chop the flesh; you need about 3 cups. Put into a food processor with the sugar, ginger, and lime juice, then blend until smooth.

Transfer the sorbet to an ice cream maker and process according to the manufacturer's directions. If you don't have an ice cream maker, put the mixture into a freezer-proof container and freeze for 2–3 hours or until ice crystals have appeared on the surface. Beat with a handheld electric mixer until smooth, then return to the freezer. Repeat this process two times until you have a fine-textured sorbet and freeze until firm.

Remove the sorbet from the freezer 10 minutes before serving. Serve, scooped in glasses with a thin cookie.

For honeydew melon granita, put ⅓ cup granulated sugar in a saucepan with ⅔ cup water and stir over low heat until dissolved, then bring to a boil. Remove from the heat and let cool, then put into a food processor with 3 cups chopped honeydew melon flesh and 2 tablespoons melon liqueur (optional) and blend until smooth. Transfer to a shallow freezer-proof container and freeze for 1 hour or until ice crystals appear at the edges. Stir the ice into the center and return to the freezer. Stir and refreeze a few more times until frozen all over. To serve, scrape the granita with a fork and serve immediately.

coffee latte custards

Serves **6**
Preparation time **20 minutes**,
 plus cooling and chilling
Cooking time **30 minutes**

2 **eggs**
2 **egg yolks**
1 (14 oz) can **condensed milk**
1 cup **strong black coffee**,
 cooled
⅔ cup **heavy cream**
unsweetened cocoa powder,
 sifted, for dusting
chocolate cookie cylinders,
 to serve (optional)

Beat together the eggs, egg yolks, and condensed milk in a bowl until just mixed. Gradually whisk in the coffee until blended.

Strain the mixture, then pour into six ½ cup greased coffee cups. Transfer the cups to a roasting pan. Pour enough hot water into the pan to come halfway up the sides of the cups, then bake in a preheated oven, at 325°F, for 30 minutes, until just set.

Lift the cups out of the water and let the custards cool, then transfer to the refrigerator and chill for 4–5 hours.

Whip the cream in a bowl until it forms soft swirls. Spoon the cream over the top of the custards, dust with a little sifted cocoa powder, and serve with chocolate cookie cylinders, if desired.

For dark chocolate custards, bring 2 cups milk and ⅔ cup heavy cream just to a boil in a saucepan. Add 7 oz semisweet chocolate, broken into pieces, and let melt. Mix 2 eggs and 2 egg yolks with ¼ cup superfine sugar or granulated sugar and ¼ teaspoon ground cinnamon, then gradually mix in the chocolate mixture and stir until smooth. Strain into small dishes and bake as above. After cooling and chilling, top with whipped cream and chocolate curls.

crunchy caramel mousse

Serves **6**

Preparation time **15 minutes**, plus cooling and chilling

5 oz **good-quality milk chocolate**, broken into pieces

¾ cup **caramel sauce (dulce de leche)**

1 cup **heavy cream**

1 (1½ oz) **bar milk chocolate with golden honeycomb toffee (sponge candy)**, coarsely chopped, plus extra to decorate

Melt the chocolate in a heatproof bowl set over a saucepan of gently simmering water, stirring occasionally, making sure that the water doesn't touch the bottom of the bowl. Let cool slightly.

Put the caramel sauce in a bowl with the cream and beat with a handheld electric mixer until the mixture starts to thicken and leaves a trail.

Stir a little of the caramel mixture into the melted chocolate, then fold the chocolate mixture into the caramel mixture until well combined. Stir in the chocolate bar.

Spoon the mixture into 6 small glasses and chill for 15–30 minutes; no longer, otherwise the honeycomb toffee will start to dissolve. Decorate with a little extra chocolate honeycomb toffee before serving.

For homemade honeycomb toffee (sponge candy), heat ⅓ cup granulated sugar and 2 tablespoons light corn syrup in a heavy saucepan over medium heat until the sugar melts, then boil the mixture until it turns a deep, golden caramel. Whisk in 1 teaspoon baking soda (this will make it foam up), then quickly pour onto an oiled baking sheet set on a cutting board. Let cool completely, then break into small pieces. Serve as a topping for ice cream.

classic lemon tart

Serves **8**

Preparation time **20 minutes**,
plus chilling and cooling

Cooking time **45–50 minutes**

1 sheet **prepared rolled
dough pie crust**, defrosted
if frozen

3 **eggs**

1 **egg yolk**

2 cups **heavy cream**

½ cup **granulated sugar**

⅔ cup freshly squeezed
lemon juice

confectioners' sugar, sifted,
for dusting

Roll out the dough thinly on a lightly floured surface and use it to line a 10 inch fluted tart pan. Prick the pastry shell with a fork and then chill in the refrigerator for 15 minutes.

Line the pastry shell with nonstick parchment paper, fill with dried macaroni or beans, and bake in a preheated oven, at 375°F, for 15 minutes. Remove the paper and macaroni or beans and bake for another 10 minutes, until crisp and golden. Remove from the oven and reduce the temperature to 300°F.

Beat together the eggs, egg yolk, cream, granulated sugar, and lemon juice in a bowl, then pour into the pastry shell.

Bake for 20–25 minutes, until the filling is just set. Let the tart cool in the pan, then dust with sifted confectioners' sugar and serve.

For mixed berries with cassis, to serve as an accompaniment, hull and halve or slice 8 oz fresh strawberries, depending on their size, and mix with 1 cup each of fresh raspberries and blueberries, 3 tablespoons sugar, and 2 tablespoons crème de cassis. Let soak for 1 hour before serving with the tart.

moroccan rice pudding

Serves 4
Preparation time **5 minutes**
Cooking time **30 minutes**

½ cup **short-grain rice**,
   washed and drained
¼ cup **granulated sugar**
2 **cinnamon sticks**
1 teaspoon **vanilla bean**
   paste or a few drops
   vanilla extract
2 cups **water**
1 (14 oz) can **evaporated**
   milk
2 teaspoons **rosewater**
⅓ cup **pistachio nuts**,
   coarsely chopped
a few **edible rose petals**
   (optional)

Put the rice, sugar, cinnamon sticks, vanilla bean paste or extract, and measured water into a saucepan and bring to a boil.

Reduce the heat and simmer the rice, uncovered, for 20 minutes, or according to the package directions. Stir in the evaporated milk and rosewater and simmer for another 10 minutes, until the rice is tender. Remove the cinnamon sticks.

Pour the rice pudding into warmed serving dishes and sprinkle with the pistachios and rose petals, if desired. Serve immediately.

For orange & cardamom rice pudding, put the washed and drained short-grain rice, the granulated sugar, measured water, the grated zest and juice of 1 orange, and 6 crushed cardamom pods into a saucepan. Bring to a boil, then reduce the heat and simmer for 25 minutes. Stir in the evaporated milk and cook for another 5 minutes, until the rice is tender. Serve decorated with toasted slivered almonds.

white choc & raspberry tiramisu

Serves **6**
Preparation time **20 minutes**

3 teaspoons **instant coffee**
½ cup **confectioners' sugar**
1 cup **boiling water**
12 **ladyfinger cookies**
1 cup **mascarpone cheese**
⅔ cup **heavy cream**
3 tablespoons **kirsch**
  (optional)
2 cups **fresh raspberries**
3 oz **white chocolate**, diced

Put the coffee and ¼ cup of the sugar in a shallow dish, pour over the measured water, and stir until dissolved.

Dip 6 ladyfingers, one at a time, into the coffee mixture, then crumble into the bottom of 6 glasses.

Combine the mascarpone with the remaining sugar in a bowl, then gradually beat in the cream until smooth. Stir in the kirsch, if using, then divide half the mixture among the glasses.

Sprinkle half the raspberries over the top of the mascarpone mixture in the glasses, then sprinkle with half the chocolate. Dip the remaining ladyfingers in the coffee mixture, crumble, and add to the glasses.

Add the remaining mascarpone mixture and whole raspberries to the glasses, finishing with a sprinkling of the remaining chocolate. Serve immediately or chill until required.

For classic tiramisu, mix the mascarpone with 3 tablespoons confectioners' sugar and the cream as above, stirring in 3 tablespoons Kahlúa coffee liqueur or brandy in place of the kirsch. Prepare the coffee-dipped ladyfinger cookes as above, then layer in one large dish with the mascarpone mixture and 3 oz diced semisweet chocolate, omitting the raspberries and white chocolate.

rhubarb & raspberry crisp

Serves **4**
Preparation time **10 minutes**
Cooking time **25 minutes**

1 lb fresh or defrosted frozen
   rhubarb, sliced
1 cup fresh or frozen
   raspberries
¼ cup firmly packed **light
   brown sugar**
3 tablespoons **orange juice**
raspberry ripple ice cream,
   to serve

Crumble topping
1⅔ cups **all-purpose flour**
pinch of **salt**
1¼ sticks **unsalted butter**,
   diced
¼ cup firmly packed **light
   brown sugar**

Make the crumble topping. Combine the flour and salt in a bowl, add the butter, and rub in with the fingertips until the mixture resembles bread crumbs. Stir in the sugar.

Mix together the fruits, the sugar, and orange juice in a separate bowl, then transfer to a greased ovenproof dish. Sprinkle the topping over the top and bake in a preheated oven, at 400°F, for about 25 minutes or until golden brown and bubbling.

Serve the crisp hot with raspberry ripple ice cream.

For apple & blackberry crisp, follow the recipe above, using 3 apples, peeled, cored, and chopped, and 3 cups fresh or frozen blackberries in place of the rhubarb and raspberries. Alternatively, you could use 7 plums, pitted and quartered, and 4 peeled, cored, and thinly sliced ripe pears.

hazelnut meringue gateau

Serves **6–8**
Preparation time **20 minutes**,
  plus cooling
Cooking time **30 minutes**

4 **egg whites**
1 ⅓ cups **superfine sugar**
½ teaspoon **white wine vinegar**
1 teaspoon **vanilla extract**
1 teaspoon **cornstarch**
1 cup **toasted hazelnuts**, ground
1 ¼ cups **heavy cream**
1 cup **fresh raspberries**
1 oz **semisweet chocolate**, melted

Brush two 8 inch round cake pans lightly with oil and line the bottoms with nonstick parchment paper.

Beat the egg whites in a large, grease-free bowl with a handheld electric mixer until they form stiff peaks. Gradually beat in the sugar until thick and glossy. Gently fold in the vinegar, vanilla extract, cornstarch, and hazelnuts.

Divide the mixture between the prepared pans and bake in a preheated oven, at 350°F for 30 minutes.

Let cool in the pans for 10 minutes, then turn out carefully onto a wire rack and peel off the paper.

Whip the cream in a bowl until it forms soft peaks. Spread over the bottom of 1 meringue and top with the raspberries, then sandwich together with the remaining meringue. Drizzle the melted chocolate over the top and chill until ready to serve.

For chocolate & raspberry meringue desserts, whip 1 ¼ cups heavy cream with 2 tablespoons confectioners' sugar in a bowl until it forms soft peaks, then stir in 2 cups Greek yogurt. Gently stir in 2 ½ cups fresh raspberries and 8 crushed meringue nests. Ripple through with ⅓ cup prepared chocolate sauce and divide among 6–8 glasses. Chill until ready to serve.

fig & honey desserts

Serves **4**

Preparation time **10 minutes**, plus chilling

6 **ripe fresh figs**, thinly sliced, plus 2 extra, cut into wedges, to decorate (optional)

2 cups **Greek yogurt**

¼ cup **honey**

2 tablespoons chopped **pistachio nuts**

Arrange the fig slices snugly in the bottom of 4 glasses or glass bowls. Spoon the yogurt over the figs and chill in the refrigerator for 10–15 minutes.

Drizzle 1 tablespoon honey over each dessert and sprinkle the pistachio nuts on top. Decorate with the wedges of fig, if desired, before serving.

For hot figs with honey, heat a ridged grill pan or large skillet over medium-high heat, and when hot, add 8 whole ripe fresh figs and cook for 8 minutes, turning occasionally, until charred on the outside. Alternatively, cook under a preheated broiler. Remove and cut in half. Divide among serving plates, top each with 1 tablespoonful of Greek yogurt, and drizzle with a little honey.

index

acknowledgments

Executive editor: Eleanor Maxfield
Editor: Joanne Wilson
Designer: Eoghan O'Brien
Copy-editor: Jo Richardson
Art direction and design: Penny Stock
Photographer: William Shaw
Home economy: Denise Smart
Stylist: Liz Hippisley
Production controller: Sarah Kramer

Photography copyright © Octopus Publishing Group Limited/William Shaw, except the following: copyright © Octopus Publishing Group 229; Frank Adam 71; Stephen Conroy 77, 81, 85, 89, 115, 119, 197, 231; Will Heap 10, 12, 15, 149, 211, 221; William Lingwood 27, 93; David Loftus 123; Neil Mersh 235; Lis Parsons 101, 111, 225; William Reavell 8, 9; Gareth Sambidge 41; William Shaw 107, 127, 183, 189, 215; Ian Wallace 97, 179.